SUPER STAIN REMOVER

SUPER STAIN REMOVER

Jack Cassimatis

APPLE

*I dedicate this book
to my dear wife, Kiki.*

CONTENTS

• •

INTRODUCTION

Running a home, keeping it clean, attractive and in good repair, depends largely on a combination of efficient routine, standard procedures and good old-fashioned elbow grease. Yet so often something extra is required. Even the smoothest-running household has its unexpected spills and stains, those unforeseen tasks that cannot be dealt with in a routine way.

Super Stain Remover was written as a quick and easy reference source for just such occasions. It contains a comprehensive list of stains and how to remove them, as well as useful suggestions for cleaning various household items and numerous other practical hints designed to save time and cut down the workload.

Magazines and newspapers often feature household hints, but it isn't always easy to find a particular one at the moment it is needed. All the information in this book is listed alphabetically, plus there is a comprehensive index, which means that the householder can find the answer to any query or problem in seconds – a particular boon in an emergency, when prompt action is essential.

STAIN REMOVAL KIT

Successful stain removal often depends on the quick application of the correct chemical or agent.

So that you may be prepared, it is suggested you store the following basic items. Most items are readily available from the supermarket; however, for ones you can't find, please refer to the **Product Description** pages 9 to 22 for information on where to purchase individual items.

THE BASICS

- Ammonia/cloudy ammonia
- Baking soda (Bicarbonate of soda)
- Bleach
- Borax
- Cream of tartar
- Eucalyptus oil
- Fuller's earth
- Glycerin
- Hydrochloric acid
- Hydrogen peroxide
- Kerosene
- Lacquer thinners
- Lemons
- Linseed oil
- Methylated spirits (or ethyl alcohol)
- Pumice powder
- Salt
- Soap
- Starch (powdered)
- Tailor's chalk (French chalk)
- Turpentine (mineral turpentine)
- Vinegar – white & malt (brown)
- Washing soda

In addition to the above, store some clean cloths and rags (old pantyhose are excellent for cleaning), plain fine steel-wool pads and clean, white blotting paper.

OTHER CLEANING INGREDIENTS USED IN THIS BOOK:

- Acetone
- All-purpose (plain) flour
- Alum
- Ammonium citrate
- Antiseptic
- Art-gum eraser
- Automobile paint-cutting compound
- Baby oil
- Baking powder
- Boric acid
- Bran
- Brass polish
- Camphor
- Carpet shampoo
- Castor oil
- Caustic soda
- Citric acid
- Citronella essential oil
- Copper sulfate
- Cornstarch (cornflour)
- Dishwashing detergent (liquid)
- Dry-cleaning fluid
- Emery powder
- Epsom salts
- Floor polish
- Furniture polish
- Gasoline (petrol)
- Gum arabic
- Laundry detergent (powder and liquid)
- Lavender essential oil
- Magnesia
- Mustard
- Nail polish (clear)
- Nail polish remover
- Olive oil
- Paint remover
- Paraffin oil
- Petroleum jelly
- Plate powder
- Powdered chalk
- Powdered milk
- Powdered size (poly vinyl alcohol)
- Quicklime
- Rubber cement
- Saddle soap
- Shaving cream
- Silver polish
- Sodium fluoride
- Sodium thiosulfate
- Sour milk
- Sugar soap
- Swimming pool chlorine
- Talcum powder
- Thinners
- Toothpaste
- Whiting
- Zinc

PRODUCT DESCRIPTION

Please note that some of the cleaning suggestions in this book require the use of chemicals that, if not used correctly, could have various harmful side effects. It is strongly suggested that where this symbol ⊗ appears in the book, you refer to these notes for the specific product and follow closely the precautions suggested.

When not being used, all chemicals should be safely locked away and stored out of the reach of children.

Purchase from your chemist the appropriate antidotes suggested on the labels of the chemicals, and keep them together with the chemicals in case of poisoning.

The following descriptions will also indicate where the specific products can be purchased.

Acetone
Acetone is a colorless liquid, commonly used as a solvent. It is available from the pharmacy or hardware store.

⊗ *Acetone* – Is highly flammable. Keep away from any naked flame and do not smoke near it.

All-Purpose (Plain) Flour
Commonly used in cooking, all-purpose (plain) flour is also handy in cleaning, polishing and as a base in pest extermination preparations. Readily available from the supermarket.

Alum
A double sulfate of aluminium and potash, used to enhance the color of some washables, and in pest removal preparations. It is available from the pharmacy.

Ammonia/Cloudy Ammonia
Ammonia is a compound gas of hydrogen and nitrogen that is dissolved in water to form a liquid. It has a sharp,

9

penetrating smell and is generally used in cleaning preparations, for polishing, and to clean soiled clothing. It is available from the supermarket, pharmacy and hardware store.

⊗ *Ammonia* – Gives off highly pungent fumes. Don't use around children or pets. Wear rubber gloves, avoid breathing the fumes and wash any splashes from your skin.

Ammonium Citrate

A water-soluble salt, composed of iron, ammonia and citric acid. It is used to clean rust from tools. Available from chemical manufacturers or photographic supply stores.

⊗ *Ammonium citrate* – Gives off highly pungent fumes. Don't use around children or pets. Wear rubber gloves and avoid breathing the fumes. Wash any splashes from your skin.

Antiseptic

Antibacterial antiseptic solutions (such as Dettol™) are not only good for cleaning cuts and scratches, but also good for cleaning vinyls, plastics and surface mold. Readily available from the pharmacy or supermarket.

Art-Gum Eraser

A good-quality eraser used around the home to rub away marks from walls, fabrics and other surfaces. Readily available from the newsagent or artist supply store.

Automobile Paint-Cutting Compound

Specialized solution that can be used to polish chrome, brass, copper and marble. It is available from automobile spare parts stores and automobile paint supply stores.

Baby Oil

A light, gentle oil, useful for removing stains from the skin and polishing delicate surfaces. Readily available from the pharmacy or supermarket.

Baking Powder

A mix of baking soda (bicarbonate of soda) and cream of tartar, this powder is useful not only in cooking, but also in cleaning china and glassware. It is readily available from the supermarket.

Baking Soda (Bicarbonate of Soda)

This is a powder that is mildly alkaline, and is therefore useful for neutralizing mild acids. It can be used as a versatile cleaner, stain remover and deodorizer. Readily available from the supermarket.

Bleach

A commercial preparation used to make fabrics and other surfaces white or colorless. It is readily available from the supermarket.

⊗ *Bleach* – Gives off pungent fumes. Don't use around children or pets. Wear rubber gloves and avoid breathing the fumes.

Borax

This is a mineral salt that occurs naturally. It is a combination of boric acid and soda, and has bleaching qualities. When dissolved in water, borax forms an alkaline antiseptic solution, and is useful as a disinfectant, detergent and water softener. Readily available from the supermarket.

⊗ *Borax* – Is poisonous. Don't use it around children or pets. Wear rubber gloves when using because it can irritate the skin and eyes, and will enter the body through broken or cracked skin.

Boric Acid

An acid used in pest removal preparations. Please note that it is not the same as borax. It is available from the pharmacy or hardware store.

⊗ *Boric acid* – Is poisonous. Don't use it around

children or pets. Wear rubber gloves when using because it can irritate the skin and eyes, and will enter the body through broken or cracked skin.

Bran
Not only good as a breakfast cereal, bran is also good for cleaning collars and in animal deterrent preparations. It is readily available from the supermarket.

Brass Polish
This product is useful for polishing not only brass, but copper and shells as well. Readily available from the supermarket.

Camphor
Derived from the camphor laurel tree, camphor is available in the form of camphor block, camphor tablets and spirits of camphor. Useful in a variety of cleaning and stain removal preparations, for storing silver and as a tick deterrent. It is available from the supermarket.

Carpet Shampoo
Used on carpets for general cleaning, and for spot cleaning after stain removal applications. Readily available from the supermarket.

Castor Oil
An oil obtained from castor seeds, commonly used as a lubricant and in restoring leather. It is available from the supermarket or pharmacy.

Caustic Soda
This is a white caustic solid, commonly used for cleaning metals and cement. It is available from the pharmacy or hardware store.

⊗ *Caustic soda* – Is very corrosive. Be aware of using around children or pets. Wear rubber gloves and avoid splashing onto skin or eyes. If an accident occurs, wash off with plenty of fresh water and see your doctor if eye is affected. Do not store in aluminum containers.

Citric Acid

An organic acid derived from citrus fruits and available as a powder. It is useful in removing deodorant stains from clothing. It is available from the supermarket.

Citronella Essential Oil

This essential oil concentrate is useful as a pest deterrent. It is available either from the supermarket or health-food store.

Copper Sulfate

This powder is made from the hydrated sulfate of the metal copper, and is used to remove mold and mildew from stone or bricks. It is available from the hardware store.

⊗ *Copper sulfate* – Is poisonous. Don't use around children or pets. Wear rubber gloves and avoid breathing the dust or fumes and contact with skin or eyes. If an accident occurs, wash with plenty of water.

Cornstarch (Cornflour)

This common flour is useful in removing stains from clothing and in polishing. It is readily available from the supermarket.

Cream of Tartar

This is a mildly acidic powder, commonly combined with baking soda to make baking powder. It is used to lift a variety of stains from such surfaces as marble, carpet, kitchenware and washables. Readily available from the supermarket.

Dishwashing Detergent (Liquid)

A versatile cleaner, useful for cleaning nonfabric surfaces around the home. Readily available from the supermarket.

Dry-Cleaning Fluid
This fluid is useful around the home for cleaning grease stains from wallpaper. It is available from chemical manufacturers.

Emery Powder
A powder made of granular minerals, usually corundum mixed with magnetite or hematite, used for grinding and polishing. It is available from the hardware store.

Epsom Salts
This powder is made from hydrated magnesium sulfate, and is useful in prewashing, washing and pest removal preparations. It is available from the pharmacy or supermarket.

Eucalyptus Oil
Distilled from the leaves of Australia's eucalyptus trees, this is an oil with a distinctive smell. It is useful as a disinfectant, and as an additive to cleaning and washing liquids for woolens. It is available from the supermarket or health-food store.

Floor Polish
This polish is useful not only for floors, but also for polishing piano keys. It is available from the supermarket.

Fuller's Earth
This is a very absorbent clay, which, when mixed with other ingredients, is used to remove oily or greasy stains. It is available from the pharmacy or hardware store.

Furniture Polish
This polish is applied as a finishing touch to furniture after stain removal and cleaning. It is available from the supermarket.

Gasoline (Petrol)

A mixture of liquid hydrocarbons, gasoline is used to fuel engines and as a solvent. It is available from the gas (service) station.

⊗ *Gasoline* – Is highly flammable. Keep away from any naked flame and do not smoke near it.

Glycerin

Glycerin is a colorless, odorless, syrupy liquid. It is good for loosening some types of stains, and is also used in a variety of other general cleaning preparations. Readily available from the supermarket.

Gum Arabic

This is a gum obtained from acacia trees, and used to sharpen creases in clothing. It is available from the pharmacy or hardware store.

Hydrochloric Acid

This is a very strong acid, used to clean heavy stains from surfaces such as cement, tiles, marble, leather, slate and metals. It is available from the hardware store.

⊗ *Hydrochloric acid* – Is highly corrosive. Be aware of using around children or pets. Wear rubber gloves and avoid splashing onto skin or eyes. If an accident occurs, wash off with plenty of running water and see your doctor if eye is affected. When mixing, use only a plastic, glass or earthenware container.

Hydrogen Peroxide

This is an oxidizing liquid, commonly used as an antiseptic and bleaching agent. It is available from the supermarket or pharmacy.

⊗ *Hydrogen peroxide* – Unless otherwise stated, must always be diluted with water. Refer to instructions on container.

Kerosene

Kerosene is a liquid obtained from distilled petroleum. It is useful in removing a variety of stains from enamel, plastic, wood, chrome, marble and fabric surfaces. Readily available from the supermarket.

⊗ *Kerosene* – Is flammable. Keep away from any naked flame.

Lacquer Thinners

Used for diluting or removing freshly applied lacquer paint from a variety of surfaces. Available from hardware stores.

⊗ *Lacquer thinners* – Extremely flammable. Keep away from any naked flame including cigarettes.

Laundry Detergent (Powder & Liquid)

Laundry detergent is useful not only in the laundry, but for spot-removing stains from fabrics, furnishings and other surfaces. A variety of powders, liquids, and fabric-specific preparations are readily available from the supermarket.

Lavender Essential Oil

Distilled from the lavender flower, pure lavender oil not only leaves a lovely fresh fragrance when added to cleaning products, but also has antibacterial properties of its own. It is available from the supermarket, pharmacy or health-food store.

Lemons

The acidic nature of this fruit makes its juice very useful as a mild bleach, disinfectant and cleaning agent. Its efficiency and strength are enhanced when used with baking soda (bicarbonate of soda). Readily available from the supermarket or produce market.

Linseed Oil

An oil pressed from the seed of flax (linseed), linseed oil is commonly used as a cleaning and polishing agent for wood and cane. It is available from the hardware or health-food store.

Magnesia – Powdered or Block

The powdered form of magnesium is used in cleaning preparations for carpets, upholstery, pearls, fur coats, woolens and sheepskin. The block form is used in removing grease stains. Both are available from the pharmacy.

Methylated Spirits

This alcohol-based liquid spirit is versatile in its use as a household cleaning agent. Readily available from the supermarket. If methylated spirits is unavailable in your area, use one of the following products in its place: ethyl alcohol, denatured alcohol, denatured ethanol or pure alcohol. Use in equal proportions as directed for methylated spirits.

⊗ *Methylated spirits* – Is highly flammable. Keep away from any naked flame and do not smoke near it.

Mustard

This condiment is useful in removing ink stains from fabrics. Readily available from the supermarket.

Nail Polish (Clear)

This clear varnish, while normally used for protecting fingernails and colored nail polish from cracking, is also great for mending tears in fabrics and stockings. Readily available from the supermarket or pharmacy.

Nail Polish Remover

This usually acetone-based liquid is very useful for removing nail polish, glue and other stains from a variety of surfaces. Readily available from the supermarket or pharmacy.

⊗ *Nail polish remover* – Is highly flammable. Keep away from any naked flame and do not smoke near it.

Olive Oil
An oil pressed from olives, olive oil is very useful as a cleaning and polishing agent, especially for wood and cane. It is readily available from the supermarket.

Paint Remover
Specialised solution used to remove paint from a variety of surfaces. It is available from the hardware store.

⊗ *Paint remover* – Gives off highly pungent fumes. Don't use it around children or pets. Wear rubber gloves and avoid breathing the fumes. Wash any splashes from your skin.

Paraffin Oil
A thick, colorless oil obtained from petroleum, useful around the home for removing grass stains, in polishing and in pest removal. Readily available from the supermarket.

Petroleum Jelly
A clear, soft substance obtained from petroleum and generally used as a base for ointments. It is useful around the house for cleaning and polishing vinyl, china, leather, rubber and wood. Readily available from the supermarket.

Plate Powder
A powder used to polish silver jewelry. It is available from the supermarket or Jeweler.

Powdered Chalk
Powdered chalk is used around the home for polishing marble. It is available from the hardware store.

Powdered Milk

Powdered milk is handy around the home for washing delicate fabrics such as lace curtains, and delicate surfaces such as piano keys. It is readily available from the supermarket.

Powdered Size (Poly Vinyl Alcohol)

Powdered size is made from glue or starch, and is used for glazing paper, cloth and other fabrics. It is useful around the home for maintaining the glazed look on curtains. It is available from the newsagent.

Pumice Powder

This is a soft, porous volcanic rock powder used in cleaning and in polishing. It is available from the hardware store or a commercial mineral supplier.

Quicklime

This is a white caustic solid prepared by calcining limestone. It is generally used in making mortar and cement, but is also useful in cleaning alabaster. It is available from the hardware store or cement supply manufacturer.

Rubber Cement

A glue of thick consistency that can be applied to a variety of surfaces, and peeled off when dry. It is useful for removing dirty marks from surfaces, such as shoes. It is available from the hardware or artist supply store.

Saddle Soap

A combination soap usually consisting of a mild soap and neat's-foot oil, used for cleaning and preserving leather. It is available from hardware stores and saddlery shops.

Salt

This white, crystalline powder has an abrasive action, and is particularly useful for cleaning and removing all kinds of food and drink stains. Readily available from the supermarket.

Shaving Cream
Shaving cream is also versatile around the home and can be used to clean diverse surfaces, such as diamonds and the fringes of blinds. It is readily available from the supermarket.

Silver Polish
Silver polish is useful not only for polishing silver, but for polishing wood and diamantés as well. It also good for cleaning the bases of irons. It is available from the supermarket.

Soap
Soap is useful around the home for washing stains from fabrics and other surfaces. Readily available from the supermarket.

Sodium Fluoride
A salt of hydrofluoric acid, used in pest removal preparations. It is available from a chemical manufacturer.
  ⊗ *Sodium fluoride* – After use, wash hands well.

Sodium Thiosulfate
A water-soluble crystalline salt, sometimes called sodium hyposulfite and commonly known as "hypo". It is used as a fixing bath for photographers and in removing iodine stains. It is available from the pharmacy or photographic supply store.
  ⊗ *Sodium thiosulfate* – After use, wash hands well.

Sour Milk
Sour or off milk is useful around the home to remove ink and mildew stains from carpet and other washable fabrics. Leave milk unrefrigerated or out in the sun to sour it.

Starch (Powdered)
Starch is found in various vegetables and made into a powder. It is commonly used in adhesives and to stiffen fabrics. It is readily available from the supermarket.

Sugar Soap
A soap substance with the appearance of brown sugar, which, when dissolved in water, gives an alkaline solution. Used to prepare walls for painting, and to remove grease stains from walls. It is available from the hardware store.

Swimming Pool Chlorine
This chlorine substance can be used diluted to clean mold from the shower recess. It is available from swimming pool supply stores.

⊗ *Swimming pool chlorine* – Gives off highly pungent fumes. Don't use around children or pets. Wear rubber gloves and avoid breathing the fumes. Wash any splashes from your skin.

Tailor's Chalk (French Chalk)
This is a soft type of limestone used by tailors to mark material. It is available from haberdashery, craft or sewing supply stores.

Talcum Powder
Powder made from the soft mineral magnesium silicate, and commonly used scented in toiletries and cosmetics. It is very useful in cleaning as a gentle abrasive agent. Readily available from the supermarket.

Thinners
Used for diluting paint or for removing freshly applied paint. Available from the hardware store.

⊗ *Thinners* – Extremely flammable. Keep away from any naked flame including cigarettes.

Toothpaste

Toothpaste has more uses around the home than for cleaning teeth. It is also useful for cleaning painted, vinyl or plastic surfaces; diamonds; and other jewelry. It is readily available from the supermarket.

Turpentine (Mineral Turpentine)

This liquid is extracted from coniferous trees and used to thin varnishes and paints. Readily available from the supermarket.

⊗ *Turpentine* – Is highly flammable. Keep away from any naked flame and do not smoke near it.

Vinegar – White & Malt (Brown)

This common cooking ingredient is equally versatile as a cleaner. Its mildly acidic properties make it useful to neutralize grease stains, fight mold, and to act as a disinfectant, bleach and deodorizer. Use white vinegar for preparations on light colored fabrics or surfaces, and malt (brown) vinegar on darker colored fabrics or surfaces. Both are readily available from the supermarket.

Washing Soda

This is a crystalline powder that makes up the greater part of laundry formulas. It is used to soften water when washing clothes. Readily available from the supermarket.

Whiting

A pure white chalk of calcium carbonate, ground, and used for making putty and cleaning china. It is available from the hardware store.

Zinc

The powdered form of the element zinc is used to remove soot from the chimney by burning it in the fireplace. It is available from the pharmacy.

PRODUCTS, PERSONAL HEALTH AND THE ENVIRONMENT

It is recommended that you should take all care when using the products and recipes throughout this book. All ingredients should be labelled and stored responsibly out of the reach of children. Some chemicals, as noted previously, are poisonous, corrosive or flammable, and will need to be used in the open air, or with all the windows open, and away from children, pets and plants, all of whom are far more vulnerable than adults to the possibly harmful effects of chemicals.

Also, be environmentally responsible when using the chemicals suggested in this book. Make sure that run-off from the use of these products does not make its way into edible gardens, children's play areas, storm drains, bushland, rivers or streams.

Be sure to dispose thoughtfully of products you no longer want to use. Those with hazard symbols should not be poured down the drain or put into the garbage. Leave them at a hazardous-waste facility. Contact your local municipal authorities for details of the nearest facility.

FUNDAMENTALS OF STAIN REMOVAL

■ The fresher the stain, the easier it is to remove.

■ Test chemicals for suitability on an unseen part of clothing or fabric, as some synthetic fibers or colors may be adversely affected.

■ When using a grease solvent, first apply it away from the stain and then work toward the center. This will help to prevent a ring forming. Only use clean cloths.

■ When using commercial products, make sure you follow the directions and manufacturer's precautions on the container.

■ Treat acids with care. Use rubber gloves.

■ Some cleaning fluids evaporate quickly and do not allow enough time to clean the stain. Overcome this problem by placing a cup, or similar, over the stain immediately after applying cleaning fluid. Let soak then proceed with cleaning.

• •

A–Z OF STAIN REMOVAL, CLEANING AND HANDY HOUSEHOLD HINTS

• •

This A–Z guide is intended to be a quick and easy reference guide for all your around-the-house needs. There are five types of entries here:

💥 Items that are frequently stained

💥 Things that cause stains

☞ Alternative methods of cleaning

☆ Handy household hints

⊗ Caution

Please refer to **Product Description** section (pp 9 to 22) for product health and safety warnings.

PLEASE NOTE

All care should be taken when using the following suggested stain removal methods on fabrics (especially oils), carpets and delicate paint finishes. In these cases, you should always test the suggested method on a small, inconspicuous area before using.

Products and preparations that carry a ⊗ symbol may be flammable, corrosive or poisonous. You should always refer to the **Product Description** section (pp 9 to 22) for product health and safety warnings before using.

A

 ## ACID

Washables

Spread ammonia on item immediately to prevent burning a hole. Rub well with ammonia and wash as usual. Washing soda can be substituted for ammonia. (⊗ *Ammonia*)

Acid on blue cloth or serge will turn red if not neutralized immediately with ammonia. If the color of the fabric is affected by the ammonia, neutralize at once with white vinegar. (⊗ *Ammonia*)

 ## ALABASTER

Cleaning

Make a paste of quicklime and water, rub it over the alabaster and leave for 30 hours. Wash off with dishwashing detergent and warm water and rinse in clean water. Polish with a soft dry cloth.

Stained

Using a cloth dampened in turpentine, rub fine pumice powder over badly stained alabaster. Wash off as above. (⊗ *Turpentine*)

 ## ALCOHOL: SPIRITS

Carpet

As quickly as possible, absorb the excess liquid and then pour soda water over the stain. Mop up with toweling, and repeat the soda water process until all traces of the stain have disappeared.

Clothes

As quickly as possible sponge with cold water followed by diluted laundry detergent.

For whites, rinse in cold water with a few drops of white vinegar added and wash as usual.

For colors, use hydrogen peroxide instead of white vinegar. If still stained when garment is dry, sponge with pure alcohol. (⊗ *Hydrogen peroxide*)

Polished Wood

Rub gently with a cloth moistened with linseed oil and use cigarette or cigar ash as a mild abrasive.

☛ Mix linseed oil and pumice powder into a thin paste. Rub in the direction of the grain and wipe off with plain linseed oil. Follow with furniture polish. May have to be repeated.

☛ Rub lightly with silver polish.

✸ ALUMINUM

Abrasive Cleaner

Grate a bar of bath soap into 1¼ cups (10 fl oz/300 ml) water and slowly heat until the soap melts and forms a jelly. Remove from heat, add ¼ cup (2 fl oz/60 ml) turpentine and, while beating with an electric mixer, slowly add 2 tablespoons fine emery powder. Store in a sealed jar and use with a soft cloth. (⊗ *Turpentine*)

Nonabrasive Cleaner

Grate a bar of bath soap into 2 cups (16 fl oz/500 ml) water and slowly heat until the soap melts and forms a jelly. Remove from heat, add ½ cup (2½ oz/65 g) borax and reheat. Remove from heat while still a jelly and beat with an electric mixer at slow speed for approximately 5 minutes. When cool, add ¾ cup (6 fl oz/180 ml) water and 2 tablespoons glycerin and beat for 2–3 minutes until fluffy. Store in a sealed jar and use with fine steel wool. This cleaner should not pit the aluminum. (⊗ *Borax*)

Polishing

Dip a dry pad of fine steel wool in all-purpose (plain) flour and rub evenly for a high polish.

☛ Sprinkle a liberal amount of cloudy ammonia onto a clean rag and rub gently over aluminum. Polish off with a soft cloth. (⊗ *Ammonia*)

✹ ALUMINUM POTS

Cleaner

Mix equal quantities of olive oil and methylated spirits and rub well with fine steel wool. Wash as usual. (⊗ *Methylated spirits*)

☛ Sprinkle cooking salt over the bottom of the pot or pan and place over low heat for about 10 minutes. Remove salt and wipe well with a paper towel. Wash as usual.

Darkened Pots

Fill the pot to three-quarters full with water, add 1 tablespoon cream of tartar and boil for about 15 minutes. Finally, remove any white residue with fine steel wool and dishwashing detergent.

☛ Fill the pot to three-quarters full with water, add any acidy fruit peelings such as lemons, oranges, apples or even rhubarb and boil for about 15 minutes. Finally, clean with fine steel wool and dishwashing detergent.

☆ ANIMAL DETERRENT

Cats, Dogs, Possums

Sprinkle pepper on the affected area.

☛ Bury bottles up to their necks in the soil and half fill with citronella essential oil.

Snails

To prevent rain from washing away snail bait, put it in a fairly large, empty food tin and lay the tin on its side on the soil. An advantage of this is that the bait may be removed when pets are around. If you're out of commercial bait, put some bran in the tin.

☛ Laying sawdust around plants is another good method of trapping snails because it prevents them from getting back into their shells.

Ants
See **Pest Removal**

✸ ARTICHOKE

Hands

Cut a lemon in half and rub your hands with the raw edge. Rinse off in cold water.

B

✸ BALL POINT
See **Felt Tip Pen; Ink, Ball Point**

✸ BAMBOO
See **Cane**

✸ BARBECUE PLATE

Dissolve $\frac{1}{2}$ cup (3 oz/90 g) caustic soda in 4 cups (32 fl oz/1 L) very hot water. Pour onto the barbecue plate and scrub with an old brush. Rinse off well. Repeat if necessary. (⊗ *Caustic soda*)

✸ BARBECUE SAUCE

Pour laundry powder into a small container and add enough hot water to make a thin paste. Dip an old toothbrush in this solution and lightly scrub the stain until clean. Rinse well with clean water.

☛ Dilute borax with a small amount of hot water and follow procedure as above. (⊗ *Borax*)

✳ BATH AND SINK

Bath Essence

Break apart 5 or 6 roses into a small saucepan, add a pinch of rosemary leaves and a pinch of salt. Cover with water, bring to a boil, let simmer gently for 1 minute and strain. Add to bath water as required.

Cleaner

Mix together equal quantities of kerosene and methylated spirits and rub over sinks, etc. with a soft cloth. (⊗ *Kerosene,* ⊗ *Methylated spirits*)

Preventing Water Ring

Make a small sachet out of cheesecloth (muslin), fill with oatmeal and leave soak in the bath to stop grease from sticking to the sides of the bath.

Removal of Water Ring

Mix 2 parts kerosene to 1 part methylated spirits and rub over the water ring with a soft cloth.
(⊗ *Kerosene,* ⊗ *Methylated spirits*)

☛ Old nylon netting or the net bags in which fruit and vegetables are sold make very effective scrubbing cloths. Wrap the netting around your usual scrubbing cloth, or put 3–5 net bags into 1 net bag, and use for scrubbing.

☼ BEER

Polished Wood

Mix linseed oil and pumice powder into a thin paste. Rub in the direction of the grain and wipe off with linseed oil. Follow with furniture polish. May have to be repeated.

Unwashables
Rub the stain with methylated spirits followed by hand soap. When dry, brush off and then sponge with cold water. (⊗ *Methylated spirits*)

Washables
Wash in warm water containing ammonia. (⊗ *Ammonia*)

BEET

Washables
Soak a slice of bread in cold water and place it over the stain. After the stain is absorbed by the bread, wash the item as usual.

BIRD DROPPINGS

Fabric
If fresh, simply wash off with water. If dry, scrape off as much as possible and remove the stain with a solution of laundry detergent and water mixed with a few drops of ammonia. Rinse off with fresh water. (⊗ *Ammonia*)

BLINDS

Fringes
Work shaving cream into a lather and apply to the fringes with a nail brush. When dry, brush off.

Holland
In a 2 gallon (8 L) bucket, add $^1/_4$ cup (1 oz/30 g) laundry powder and $^1/_2$ cup (4 fl oz/125 ml) kerosene and then fill the bucket three-quarters full with warm water. Stir well. Remove the blind from the window and lay out on a clean, flat surface. With a soft cloth, apply the mixture all over the blind on both sides, wiping each side with a clean cloth as it is finished. (⊗ *Kerosene*)

Venetian

Cleaning very dirty venetian blinds

In a 2 gallon (8 L) bucket, pour $^1/_4$ cup (1 oz/30 g) laundry powder and $^1/_2$ cup (4 fl oz/125 ml) kerosene and then fill the bucket three-quarters full with warm water. Stir well. Remove the blind from the window and lay out on a clean, flat surface. Dip a soft broom or a sponge mop into the solution and scrub the blinds, including the pelmet, tapes and cords. Apply to both sides. When clean, hang the blinds over the clothesline and rinse with water from a hose. Leave to dry. ($\otimes$ *Kerosene*)

Cleaning without removing from windows

Wipe each slat with a cloth that is lightly dampened with kerosene. Polish with a dry cloth.
($\otimes$ *Kerosene*)

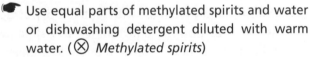 Use equal parts of methylated spirits and water or dishwashing detergent diluted with warm water. ($\otimes$ *Methylated spirits*)

 ## BLOOD

Carpet

Sponge the stain with diluted laundry detergent and then with clean water. If any stain remains, rub with a cloth dampened with hydrogen peroxide. Sponge with clean water. Never allow the hydrogen peroxide to saturate the carpet.
($\otimes$ *Hydrogen peroxide*)

Colors

Rub the stain lightly with hydrogen peroxide.
($\otimes$ *Hydrogen peroxide*)

Unwashables

Mix cornstarch (cornflour) or starch with water until thick and spread it over the stain. Wait until dry and then brush off. May need repetition.

White Washables

Soak the item in cold salted water, using 1 tablespoon salt to 2$\frac{1}{2}$ cups (20 fl oz/625 ml) water, then wash as usual.

☛ Use bleach as per directions on container. ($\otimes$ *Bleach*)

✳ BOOKS

Top Edge of Pages

Rub away dirt with an art-gum eraser. If still soiled, rub gently with a dry pad of fine steel wool.

✳ BOTTLES

Hard-to-Get-into Bottles

Pour a small amount of white or malt (brown) vinegar into the bottle and add crushed eggshells and hot water. Shake very well and leave for a day or so. Shake every now and then and if still stained, clean with fine steel wool tied to a thin stick.

☛ Tie a thin chain onto a piece of string, drop the chain into the bottle with hot water and dishwashing detergent seal the bottle and shake well. When clean, remove the chain and rinse well.

✳ BRASS

Polishing

Use ordinary brass polish or automobile paint-cutting compound. Apply with a soft cloth or, if necessary, with a pad of fine steel wool. Rub only in straight lines, not crosswise or in circles. When dry, remove the polish with a silk cloth, and for a really high gleam, rub with all-purpose (plain) flour. Flour removes all traces of polish and helps to maintain the shine.

See also **Tarnish, Brass**

✺ BRICKS

See **Cement; Mildew; Oil; Paint**

✺ BROILER (GRILLER)

Use a container large enough to hold the broiler (griller) grid. A metal laundry tub is ideal. Pour in boiling water and $1/2$ cup (3 oz/90 g) caustic soda. Mix well, immerse grid and let soak for at least 15 minutes. Wearing rubber gloves, scrub the grid with a wire brush or scrubbing brush. Rinse well under running water. Treatment may have to be repeated. (⊗ *Caustic soda*)

✺ BURNS: CIGARETTE

Carpet

While the burn cannot be removed, it can be hidden by rubbing around it with steel wool. This will lift the carpet fibers and cover the mark.

 Remove all burn marks by rubbing carefully with steel wool or sandpaper. Next, pour into the burn hole a small amount of clear, waterproof adhesive and, using a pair of fine-pointed tweezers, pluck fragments of pile from the surrounding carpet and push them into the adhesive. When dry, tease the patch with a small wire brush to remove any glazing effect.

Fabric

Darn the hole with matching tapestry, crocheting or wool thread.

Polished Wood

Mix fine pumice powder and linseed oil into a thin paste. Rub over the burn mark in the direction of the grain. Wipe off with a clean cloth dipped in linseed oil. Repeat if necessary. Finish off with furniture polish.

Upholstery

Mix 4 tablespoons borax with 2 cups (16 fl oz/ 500 ml) hot water. Dampen a rag with this solution and rub over the burn mark until it disappears. Sponge off with clean water and pat dry. (⊗ *Borax*)

 ## BURNS: POTS, PANS, DISHES

Method 1

Pour in hot water and 1 tablespoon bleach and let soak. All food particles should then come off easily in the wash. For burnt caked-on food, place the pot or pan on the stove and let boil for 10 minutes or more. (⊗ *Bleach*)

☞ For old and very stubborn, baked-on grease, saturate an old rag with ammonia and put it with the pot or pan in a plastic bag. Seal the bag and leave for a day or so. Wash as usual. (⊗ *Ammonia*)

NOTE:

Method 1 may cause pitting on new aluminum.

Method 2

Fill the pot three-quarters full with cold water and leave to soak for 30 minutes. Add 1 heaped tablespoon borax and boil for about 10 minutes. Wash as usual. (⊗ *Borax*)

Method 3

Sprinkle salt, baking soda (bicarbonate of soda) or coffee grounds over the bottom of the pot, cover with white or malt (brown) vinegar and let stand for at least 1 hour. Then add a small amount of water, boil for 10 minutes and wash as usual.

C

 CANDLE WAX

Furniture

Wait until the drops of wax become hard (a few hours). Place a large sheet of aluminum foil over drops and then place a hot steamy towel on top of this. If furniture is polished wood, do not let the towel touch the woodwork. When sufficiently heated, the wax should soften and you can peel it off.

See also **Wax**

 CANE, BAMBOO

Cleaning Liquid

Mix the following:

- $1^1/4$ cups (10 fl oz/300 ml) turpentine
- $^3/4$ cup (6 fl oz/180 ml) linseed oil
- $^1/2$ cup (4 fl oz/125 ml) white vinegar
- $^3/4$ cup (6 fl oz/180 ml) methylated spirits

Rub cleaning liquid thoroughly over the cane or bamboo and dry off with a clean cloth. When dry, restore gloss by painting all over with clear lacquer. ($\otimes$ *Turpentine*, $\otimes$ *Methylated spirits*)

Quick Cleaning

Make a solution of 1 tablespoon ammonia and 1 tablespoon salt mixed with 4 cups (32 fl oz/1 L) water. Scrub the cane or bamboo with the solution, and then rinse off with clean water. Let dry in the shade. When dry, finish off with furniture polish. ($\otimes$ *Ammonia*)

CARBON PAPER

Fabric

Sponge the stain with methylated spirits.
($\otimes$ *Methylated spirits*)

CARDS: PLAYING

Wipe each card with spirits of camphor and let dry. When dry, sprinkle talcum powder over each card and polish with a soft cloth. An occasional dusting of talcum powder will remove surface grease and reduce the number of cleanings required.

CARPET

Brightening Old Carpet

First, clean the carpet thoroughly with a vacuum cleaner. Then mix a solution of 1 cup (8 fl oz/250 ml) white vinegar and 1 teaspoon laundry detergent for each 2 cups (16 fl oz/500 ml) water used. Apply the solution with a sponge. Leave to dry before walking on the carpet.

Cleaning

Sprinkle baking soda (bicarbonate of soda) all over the carpet, rub in well with a scrubbing brush or straw broom and leave overnight. Next day, vacuum the carpet. Instead of baking soda, you can use powdered magnesia or damp salt.

☞ Mix a solution of $^1/_2$ cup (4 fl oz/125 ml) white vinegar to $2^1/_2$ cups (20 fl oz/625 ml) water. Add more vinegar for persistent stains. Scrub the solution into the carpet, let dry and then vacuum the carpet.

☞ Mix a solution of 4 tablespoons baking soda (bicarbonate of soda), 2 tablespoons ammonia, $^1/_4$ cup (2 fl oz/60 ml) laundry detergent and

2$\frac{1}{2}$ cups (20 fl oz/625 ml) water. Mix well and apply with a soft brush. Wipe off excess liquid, leave to dry thoroughly. (⊗ *Ammonia*)

☛ Mix laundry detergent and a small amount of water and beat well with a mixer until the suds become thick and creamy. Apply with a soft brush in the direction of the pile and wipe up the dirty suds. Finish off by going over the carpet once or twice with a clean cloth that has been dipped in warm water and squeezed dry.

Flat Spots

Hold a steam iron as close to the carpet as possible without touching it. The steam will bring up the pile. Straighten the pile with a coarse comb or brush.

Intermittent Stain

If you have a mysterious stain on your carpet that appears in damp weather and disappears again in dry weather, it is probably caused by salt or sugar. Choose a dry day and vacuum the carpet thoroughly, then sponge the area with warm water and laundry detergent. Dry well with a cloth, and when the carpet is completely dry, vacuum again.

 ## CEMENT

Bricks

Tap lumps of dried cement lightly with a hammer, and then scraped off with a stiff wire brush or a broken, flat piece of brick.

Clean off the gray residue by scrubbing with a stiff brush dipped in a solution of 1 part hydrochloric acid to 8 parts water, being careful not to get any on the mortar between the bricks. Leave to soak for 10 minutes. Rinse off with the hose and repeat the procedure until the stain is removed. (⊗ *Hydrochloric acid*)

Tiles

Mix a solution of 1 part hydrochloric acid to 8 parts water. Apply with an old brush and leave to soak for 10 minutes. Rinse off with clean water. Make sure that none of the solution gets into the cement joints between the tiles. ($\otimes$ *Hydrochloric acid*)

✳ CERAMIC TILES

Rub the stain with a cloth dipped in white vinegar. See also **Cement, Tiles; Rust**

✳ CHAIR UPHOLSTERY

Padded

A dry foam rubber sponge, rubbed over the fabric, will remove the loose dirt and enhance the colors. To remove grime that has accumulated over a long period, sprinkle all over with powdered magnesia and rub in well. Leave overnight, then brush off with a soft brush.

Replacing Button

Insert an ordinary hairpin through the eye in the back of the button and open out the hairpin. Bring the opened ends together, push them through the hole in the back of the chair and let go. The hairpin will spring out and hold the button in place.

Vinyl

Regular cleaning with dishwashing detergent will keep the material clean. To maintain the new look, rub in a small amount of petroleum jelly and polish off with a soft cloth.

WARNING:

Do not use solvent-type cleaners on upholstery that contains foam, rubber, or plastic padding, as the padding may be damaged.

CHAYOTE (CHOKO)

Hands

Cut a raw potato in half and rub your hands with the raw edge. Rinse off in cold water.

 CHERRY

Washables

Rub the stain with a cut ripe tomato. Wash as usual.

 CHINA

Dull

Rub thoroughly with petroleum jelly. Leave for 1 hour, then polish off with a clean cloth.

Stained Cracks

Dampen the cracks and then rub in baking powder. Leave for 2 hours, then wash and rinse as usual. Repeat if necessary.

 CHOCOLATE

Unwashables

Sponge with methylated spirits and then clean using the mixture for Washables. ($\otimes$ *Methylated spirits*)

Vinyl

Clean off with hot water followed by methylated spirits. ($\otimes$ *Methylated spirits*)

Washables

Soak the article in a mixture of 4 tablespoons borax and 2^{1}/$_{2}$ cups (20 fl oz/625 ml) warm water. Wash as usual. ($\otimes$ *Borax*)

 CHROME

Cleaning

Sprinkle methylated spirits on a clean cloth and rub it over the chrome. ($\otimes$ *Methylated spirits*)

Heavy Grime

Spread a liberal amount of automobile paint-cutting compound over the chrome and buff with a buffing or lamb's wool pad fitted to an electric drill.

Light Rust

Rub the chrome lightly but briskly with a new pad of dry fine steel wool. If necessary, use a small amount of kerosene with the steel wool. (⊗ *Kerosene*)

Small Items

Small chrome items can be cleaned and polished at the same time by rubbing them with an art-gum eraser.

COCONUT OIL

Place the stain over blotting paper and rub well with tailor's chalk. Leave for 12 hours and brush off.

COFFEE

Carpet

Mix borax with warm water and rub the stain with a cloth soaked in this solution. (⊗ *Borax*)

Cotton and Linen

Ensure first that the material and material dye will withstand boiling water.

Dab glycerin on the stain and leave for 15 minutes. Then spread the stained area over a saucepan or bowl and, from a height of $1^{1}/_{2}$–3 ft (45cm–1 m), pour boiling water through the cloth.

For an old stain, spread on a mixture of borax and water. Leave for 15 minutes and wash as usual. (⊗ *Borax*)

Marble

First, clean the marble as suggested under **Marble** (p 78), then apply the following poultice:

41

Mix equal quantities of hydrogen peroxide, ammonia and cream of tartar and add sufficient whiting or flour to make a paste. Spread thickly over the stain and cover with plastic wrap to keep moist. Leave for 10 hours or more, then remove plastic and leave to dry. When dry, brush off and clean with dishwashing detergent and water. Repeat if necessary. (⊗ *Hydrogen peroxide,* ⊗ *Ammonia*)

Unwashables
Sponge with a solution of 4 tablespoons borax to $2^1/2$ cups (20 fl oz/625 ml) water followed by methylated spirits. (⊗ *Borax,* ⊗ *Methylated spirits*)

Vacuum Bottle
Make a solution of $^1/3$ cup (2 oz/60 g) baking soda (bicarbonate of soda) to $2^1/2$ cups (20 fl oz/625 ml) water. Pour into vacuum bottle and shake well. Leave for 10 minutes. Wash as usual.

Washables
Soak the item in a solution of 4 tablespoons borax to $2^1/2$ cups (20 fl oz/625 ml) water, then wash as usual. (⊗ *Borax*)

Woolens
Mix glycerin with egg yolk and spread over the stain. Leave for 30 minutes. Wash in warm water.

 ## COLORS
To enhance the colors of washables, the following are suggested:

Black, Navy, Bone/Fawn, Brown
Add 1 teaspoon malt (brown) vinegar to the washing water.

Blue
Add a small amount of salt to the washing water.

Green, Mauve
Add a small amount of alum to washing water.

Pink, Red
Same as Black and add a few drops of cochineal or red ink to the final rinse water.

Cotton Colors
Add $1/4$ cup (2 fl oz/60 ml) malt (brown) vinegar to final rinse water.

✸ COMPUTER

Keyboard
Brush the keyboard with a clean, soft-hair, paintbrush, then remove dust and dirt with a soft, dry cloth. If keys are stained, sprinkle a few drops of dishwashing detergent on a damp cloth, wring the cloth so that it is as dry as possible, and lightly rub over the stained keys. Ensure that no water is released into the keyboard. Wipe over with a dry cloth.

Screen
With the same moist cloth used to clean the keyboard, wipe over the screen and then dry the screen with a clean, soft cloth.

✸ COPPER

Finger Plates, Knobs, etc.
Use ordinary brass polish.

Polishing
You can use ordinary brass polish or automobile paint-cutting compound. If the copper is not too dull, apply with a soft cloth. However, if badly tarnished, apply with a pad of fine steel wool. Rub only in straight lines, not crosswise or in circles. Finally, remove polish with a soft cloth and buff to a high gleam with cotton wool.

See also **Tarnish, Copper**

Pots

Mix 1 tablespoon salt with 2 tablespoons white or malt (brown) vinegar and, using a soft cloth, rub the mixture over the copper pot. Rinse in hot water and dry thoroughly.

Utensils

Cut a lemon in half, dip the cut edge in salt and rub over the copper utensil. Wash and rinse as usual.

WARNING:

Do not use the above suggestions on simulated copper.

 ## CORRECTION FLUID/LIQUID PAPER

To remove dried correction fluid from paper or material, place a few drops of correction fluid thinner (available from stationery stores) on a small cloth and rub onto the dried fluid. May require more than one application of thinner.

☛ You could also use methylated spirits in place of thinner. (⊗ *Methylated spirits*)

 ## COSMETICS

Marble

Treat as for **Cream, Ice Cream, Marble**

Unwashables

Sponge with eucalyptus oil.

Washables

Soak the item in a solution of 1 teaspoon ammonia to 2$\frac{1}{2}$ cups (20 fl oz/625 ml) warm water. Wash as usual. (⊗ *Ammonia*)

 ## CRAYON

Paint

Rub with toothpaste, leave for 15 minutes and then wash off.

Wallpaper

Spread a sheet of blotting paper over the area and rub with a hot iron. May require repetition.

CREAM, ICE CREAM

Marble

First, clean the marble as suggested under **Marble** (p 78). Then mix equal quantities of methylated spirits and acetone and add sufficient whiting or flour to make a paste. Apply the paste following the directions for **Coffee, Marble**.

(⊗ *Methylated spirits,* ⊗ *Acetone)*

Unwashables

Clean with methylated spirits and when dry, sponge with warm water. (⊗ *Methylated spirits*)

Washables

Soak the item in warm water and wash as usual.

CREASES

Following are various methods to sharpen creases or pleats and make them last longer.

1. Rub a piece of damp soap on the inside of the crease. Iron the crease on the outside using a damp cloth.
2. For dark fabric, place a cloth dampened with cold tea over the crease and then iron the crease.
3. Dampen the crease with water mixed with a small amount of gum arabic.

Crease Resisting of Garments

Dissolve 1 level tablespoon gelatin in a small amount of hot water and add to the final rinse water. Dry as normal.

Removing Stubborn Creases

Make a solution of 2 tablespoons epsom salts and 5 cups (40 fl oz/1.25 L) warm water. Mix well and soak the creased garment for approximately 4 hours. Dry as normal without wringing. Finish off with a steam iron.

☞ Make a solution of $^3/_4$ cup (6 fl oz/180 ml) methylated spirits, 2 cups (16 fl oz/500 ml) white vinegar and 5 cups (40 fl oz/1.25 L) warm water. Mix well and soak the creased garment for approximately 4 hours or until the crease disappears. Wash as usual, rinse and dry. (⊗ *Methylated spirits*)

✳ CRYSTAL GLASSWARE

For sparkling glassware, half fill your kitchen sink with warm water, add 1 cup (8 fl oz/250 ml) white vinegar and let glassware soak for 15 minutes. If necessary, clean the grooves in the crystal with a toothbrush. Rinse off with clean, warm water.
See also **Jewelry**

✳ CURRY

Dilute borax with a small amount of hot water and rub it over the stain with a toothbrush. Remove any residue with white vinegar. (⊗ *Borax*)

✳ CURTAINS

Glazed Chintz

To retain the glazed look, wash and rinse as usual. Then, in a saucepan, bring 5 cups (40 fl oz/1.25 L) water to a boil, add 6 tablespoons powdered size and simmer, stirring continuously, until the size is fully dissolved. Strain well and when cool, immerse the curtains in the solution. To dry, let the excess solution drip off, then roll up the curtains in an old towel. Do not hang on the clothesline. When nearly dry, iron the curtains on the wrong side with a cool dry iron and on the right side with a fairly hot dry iron.

Lace, Nylon and Net

Because of their delicacy, it is advisable to wash these fabrics by hand in warm water and, for a crisp finish add to the final rinse $^1/2$ cup (2 oz/60 g) powdered milk for white curtains or $^1/2$ cup (1 oz/30 g) bran for tinted curtains.

☞ Add 1 tablespoon methylated spirits to the final rinse water. ($\otimes$ *Methylated spirits*)

Plastic

Plastic curtains can be washed successfully in the washing machine. If they are stained, add 2 tablespoons liquid bath cleaner to the washing water. Do not spin-dry as it will crease the curtains.

Plastic Shower

Mix $^1/4$ cup (2 fl oz/60 ml) kerosene in 2 gallons (8 L) hot water, immerse the curtain and leave for 30 minutes. Rinse in hot water and hang, full length, on the clothesline to dry. ($\otimes$ *Kerosene*)

✺ CUTLERY

Drying/Polishing Cloth

Dissolve 2 tablespoons whiting in $2^1/2$ cups (20 fl oz/625 ml) water. Soak a tea towel in this mixture, hang to dry and then use only when drying cutlery. Wash the tea towel in the same mixture.

General Stain Remover

Fill a wide mouthed jar three-quarters full with water, add 2 teaspoons salt and drop in some silver paper or aluminum foil. Keep the jar near the sink and, when required, place tarnished or stained cutlery into the mixture and leave for at least 10 minutes. Wash and rinse cutlery as usual. Replace the silver paper or aluminum foil frequently.

Ivory or Bone Handles

Restore the handles by rubbing them with a cloth dipped in hydrogen peroxide. Rinse well.
($\otimes$ *Hydrogen peroxide*)

☞ Cut a lemon in half, dip it in salt and rub it over the handles. Rinse well.

☞ For badly stained handles, soak for 5 minutes or more in a solution of equal parts of water and bleach. Rinse well.

Silver Cutlery

To remove stains, dip a damp cloth in baking soda (bicarbonate of soda) and rub it over the cutlery. Wash as usual.

☞ Cut a potato in half and rub the raw edge over the cutlery.

See also **Silver**

Stainless Steel Cutlery

To remove stains, dip a damp cloth in flour and rub it over the cutlery. Wash as usual.

D

✳ DENTURES

Soak dentures for 30 minutes in a solution of 2 tablespoons white vinegar and 1 cup (8 fl oz/ 250 ml) water.

✳ DEODORANT

Dab the stain with laundry detergent followed by white vinegar. When stain is removed, dab with clean warm water. If it is a stubborn stain, leave to soak in detergent for approximately 5 hours. If the stain remains, soak it in a solution of $2^1/3$ oz (70 g) citric acid to $1^2/3$ cups (13 fl oz/400 ml) hot water. If the stain is still a problem, rub some citric acid powder directly onto it and rinse off well.

✳ DIAPERS (NAPPIES)

Remove as much of the excess as possible, then soak the item in cold water mixed with a small amount of white vinegar for approximately 1 hour. Rinse well.

☆ DUSTING CLOTH FOR POLISHED WOOD

Soak a cloth in turpentine, kerosene or paraffin oil, wring and hang to dry. Apart from being better than an ordinary cloth, it also buffs the polish and leaves the timber more gleaming. Re-treat as necessary. ($\otimes$ *Turpentine*, $\otimes$ *Kerosene*)
See also **Furniture**

✳ DYE

Clothing

Saturate the spot with lemon juice and brush in sufficient cornstarch (cornflour) to make a thick paste. When dry, brush off and wash as usual.

If unsuccessful, try bleaching white clothes with bleach and colored clothes with hydrogen peroxide; and then add a few drops of ammonia to the rinse water. ($\otimes$ *Bleach*, $\otimes$ *Hydrogen peroxide*, $\otimes$ *Ammonia*)
See also **Hair Rinse (Dye)**

E

 EGG

Carpet

Scrape off the excess and lightly soak the stain with a solution of 1 tablespoon white vinegar and 2 tablespoons laundry detergent to 2 cups (16 fl oz/500 ml) warm water. Pat dry. Repeat if necessary.

Cutlery

Dip a damp cloth in coarse salt and rub it over the stains to remove them.

 Place stained cutlery in the water used to boil the eggs, leave for 10 minutes and the stain will easily wash off.

Unwashables

Spread warm soap suds onto the stain and when dry, clean off with methylated spirits.
($\otimes$ *Methylated spirits*)

Washables

Wash off as much as possible in cold salted water followed, when dry, by a commercial stain remover.

 EMBROIDERY GUIDELINES

Dampen a rag with methylated spirits and rub it over the guidelines until they disappear. Wash as usual. ($\otimes$ *Methylated spirits* – Always test on a corner of the fabric first as some synthetics may be damaged by methylated spirits).

ENAMEL POTS, ETC.

Fill the pot three-quarters full with water, add any acidic fruit peelings such as lemons, oranges, apples or rhubarb and boil for 15 minutes. Pour off the boiling water and immediately pour in a small amount of cold water. Leave for 5 minutes and then wash as usual.

☞ Place 4 raw, unwashed potatoes in the pot, cover potatoes with water, bring to a boil and simmer until the water has nearly evaporated. Re-cover potatoes with water, re-boil and simmer until the water has nearly evaporated again. Repeat this procedure four times and then let stand overnight. Wash as usual.

✹ **EXHAUST FAN FILTER: METALLIC**

Place the filter on some old newspaper in strong sunlight, and leave for a few hours until the grease melts and runs off. If further cleaning is required, make a solution of $1/2$ cup (3 oz/90 g) caustic soda dissolved in 1 gallon (4 L) warm water. Place the filter in the solution and brush it over the filter with an old brush. Rinse off with plenty of cold water and leave to dry. (⊗ *Caustic soda*)

E–F

F

✹ **FELT TIP PEN**

Thoroughly wet a cloth in methylated spirits, turpentine or kerosene. Dab the stain, ensuring that you always use a clean area of the cloth. Rub with glycerin if surface becomes dull.

(⊗ *Methylated spirits,* ⊗ *Turpentine,* ⊗ *Kerosene*)

☞ Some shampoos are also effective in removing this type of stain, as is eucalyptus oil.

51

FELT TIP PEN: DRIED OUT

Water-Based Pen

Remove the cap at the base of the pen and pour in a few drops of water.

Waterproof Pen

Remove the cap at the base of the pen and pour in a few drops of methylated spirits, turpentine or kerosene. (⊗ *Methylated spirits*, ⊗ *Turpentine*, ⊗ *Kerosene*)

 FERTILIZERS FOR PLANTS

Fish Tank Water

Next time you change the water in the fish tank, use it for watering indoor plants.

Milk Bottle Water

Milk bottle rinse water is a good fertilizer for maidenhair ferns.

Potato Water

Save the water used to boil potatoes (if it's not too salty). Allow to cool and use it to water your indoor plants. It waters and fertilizes at the same time.

Tea

Brewed tea is a good fertilizer; however, use only the liquid, as the leaves harden on the ground and harbor pests.

 FINGER MARKS

Rub the marks with a cloth dipped in dishwashing detergent.

 FISH ODOR

Hands

Sprinkle salt on your hands and then rub them with a cut lemon or lemon juice.

☞ Wet hands and rub with a small amount of baking soda (bicarbonate of soda).

FISH STAINS

Soak fabric with pure glycerin and leave for 4 hours. Wash as usual.

✹ FLOORS

Concrete

DUST FREE

Make a solution of 1 cup (8 fl oz/250 ml) liquid floor polish to 4 cups (32 fl oz/1 L) hot water. Mix well and use an old mop or a rag tied around a broom to coat the concrete all over.

RENEWING

Wash concrete with soap and water, rinse off with clean water and, while still wet, sprinkle on dry cement. Leave for 1–2 hours, then sweep clean of all cement powder. Rinse with clean water.

Terrazzo

STAINS

Cut a lemon in half, dip the raw edge in salt and rub it over the stain. Leave for 1–2 hours, then rinse off with clean water.

Wooden Polished

NON-SLIP POLISH

Mix together 2 tablespoons floor polish, 1 oz (30 g) piece of bar soap and ³/4 cup (6 fl oz/180 ml) boiling water. Stir well to dissolve soap and when cold, add ¹/2 cup (4 fl oz/125 ml) kerosene. Add the mixture to 5 cups (40 fl oz/1.25 L) cold water and stir well. Apply to polished floor as usual and leave to dry overnight before buffing. (⊗ Kerosene)

☞ Mix a bottle of your usual polish with ¹/4 cup (2 fl oz/60 ml) gasoline (petrol). Apply as usual, leave to dry thoroughly and then buff well for a non-slip finish. (⊗ *Gasoline*)

POLISHING

Clean and polish at the same time by adding 2 tablespoons silicone-type commercial floor wax to 2$\frac{1}{2}$ cups (20 fl oz/625 ml) boiling water. Mix well, and apply to floor. When dry rub with a soft cloth to bring up the shine.

STAINS

First, try removing the stains with a cloth dampened with a small amount of turpentine. If unsuccessful, sprinkle turpentine on a pad of fine steel wool and rub it gently over the stain in the direction of the grain. Polish any dull spots with regular floor polish and buff well. (⊗ *Turpentine*)

 FLOWERS

Prolonging the Life of Cut Flowers

The following flowers do not require any special preparation before placing in the vase. Every 3 days, trim $\frac{1}{4}$ in (6 mm) off the stems and change the water:

• Begonias, camellias, carnations, clematis, cosmos, daffodils, gardenias, gladiolus, gypsophila (don't cut, pull out with roots and all), hyacinths, marguerites, narcissi, nasturtiums, orchids, petunias, snapdragons, tulips, verbena, violets, and waterlilies.

The following flowers should have the ends of the stems scalded to a depth of 2 in (5 cm) by placing the ends in boiling water for 1 minute. Every 3 days, trim $\frac{1}{4}$ in (6 mm) off the stems and repeat. Scalding the stems prevents them from drying out:

• Asters, azaleas, cherry blossoms, chrysanthemums,

dahlias, daisies, delphiniums, forget-me-nots, fuchsias, hollyhocks, hydrangeas, Iceland poppies, irises, larkspurs, marigolds, peonies, poinsettias, poppies, primroses, roses, ranunculuses, stocks, sweet peas, wattle, and zinnias.

The following flowers should have the ends of the stems crushed. Every 3 days, change the water, cut $1/4$ in (6 mm) off the stems and recrush the ends. Crushing of hard stems allows much quicker absorption of water:

• Apple blossoms, cherry blossoms, chrysanthemums, delphiniums, hydrangeas, lilacs, lilies, November lilies, peach blossoms, peonies, roses, stocks, and tiger lilies.

The following flowers should have the stems split $1^1/2$ in (4 cm) up from the end to allow a greater volume of water to be absorbed. Every 3 days, change the water, cut $1/4$ in (6 mm) off the stems and resplit them:

• Fuchsias, lilacs, and lilies.

The following flowers will benefit from the addition of 2 tablespoons sugar to the water in the vase.

• Asters, carnations, cosmos, delphiniums, marigolds, peonies, petunias, and sweet peas.

The following flowers will benefit from the addition of 2 tablespoons white or malt (brown) vinegar to the water in the vase:

• Anemones, gladioli, and lilies.

The following flowers will benefit from the addition of 2 tablespoons salt to the water in the vase:

• Begonias, hollyhocks, marguerites, poinsettias, roses, snapdragons, stocks, violets, and wattle.

FLOWER STAINS

Hands

Mix together equal parts of butter and sugar and rub the mixture over your hands until the stains disappear. Wash with soap and water.

 FLY SPOTS

Ceiling and Walls

These may be washed off with warm water and dishwashing detergent, but the job will be easier if you wait for a rainy day. The dampness in the air will soften the spots.

 FOOD

Unwashable Surfaces

Sponge with a solution of 2 tablespoons laundry detergent, 2 tablespoons white vinegar and 2 cups (16 fl oz/500 ml) warm water. Pat dry and sponge with clean water.

✳ FRAMES

Gilt

CLEAN

Mix equal quantities of methylated spirits and ammonia and apply to dust-free frame with a soft, clean paintbrush. Leave for 10 minutes, then wipe off with a soft cloth. Do not rub too hard and do not worry if the frame is slightly sticky, as it will dry out in a day or so. (⊗ *Methylated spirits,* ⊗ *Ammonia*)

☛ Warm a bottle of turpentine by placing it in a container of very hot water (not boiling). Sprinkle warmed turpentine onto a cloth and wipe gently over the frame. Wipe off with a soft cloth. Do not worry if the frame is slightly sticky as it will dry out in a day or so. (⊗ *Turpentine*)

WARNING:

Turpentine is highly flammable and must not be placed near or on any flame or heat source, whether electric or gas. Heat the water and pour it into a suitable container, keeping the bottle of turpentine well away from the flame.

☛ Boil some onions and reserve the water. Using a soft cloth, rub the frames with the onion water. When clean, dry off with a soft cloth.

☛ Cut a fresh onion in half and rub the raw edge over the frame. Wipe off immediately with a damp cloth and finish off with a soft , dry cloth.

POLISHING

Protect and polish gilt frames by occasionally rubbing a few drops of baby oil over them and then polishing with a soft cloth.

 FRUIT AND FRUIT JUICE

Carpet

As quickly as possible, absorb excess liquid, sponge the stain with water and pat dry. If the stain remains, sponge with a solution of 2 teaspoons ammonia to $3^{1}/2$ cups (28 fl oz/875 ml) water. Finally sponge with water and pat dry. (⊗ *Ammonia*)

Clothes

Ensure first that fabric will withstand boiling water. Spread the stained area over a saucepan or similar and, from a height of $1^{1}/2$–3 ft (45cm–1 m), pour boiling water through it. When the stain is removed, wash as usual.

If the stain is old, spread on a mixture of borax and water. Leave for 15 minutes and wash as usual. (⊗ *Borax*)

☛ If washable, soak in a solution of 4 tablespoons borax to $2^{1}/2$ cups (20 fl oz/625 ml) warm water. Wash as usual. (⊗ *Borax*)

If unwashable, sponge with cold water followed by glycerin. Let stand for 1 hour, then sponge with lemon juice. Rinse off.

☞ Wet a camphor block and rub it over the stains. Wash as usual.

Marble
Treat as for **Coffee, Marble**

Temporary Action
As a temporary measure until you can treat the stain, sprinkle salt all over it.

✷ FUR

Coats
Using a firm but not too stiff brush, work in some dry, uncooked cornmeal. Let stand for at least 4 hours, then brush again well. Shake to remove all the cornmeal and brush down with a clean brush.

Collars
Heat some bran in the oven and work it into the collar with a soft brush. When clean, shake to remove all the bran and brush with a clean brush.

White Fur Coat
Treat the same as for **White Woolens**, but do not dampen fur before applying powdered magnesia and, of course, do not rinse afterward. Just shake the coat to remove all the powdered magnesia. If the fur is thick, leave the item rolled up for at least 3–4 days.

✷ FURNITURE: WOODEN

Antique
Mix together equal parts of linseed oil, turpentine and vinegar (white vinegar for light colors, malt (brown) vinegar for darker colors). Using a clean

cloth, thoroughly rub the mixture all over the furniture. Finish with a dry cloth. (⊗ *Turpentine*)

☞ Brown or clear shoe polish is also very good for polishing antique furniture.

Applying Polish

Furniture polish will be more effective if it is warm and applied with a damp cloth rather than a dry one. Polish off with a clean, dry pair of pantyhose.

To warm polish, stand the bottle in a bowl of hot water. (⊗ Do not heat aerosol cans, as they can explode and cause injury.)

Do not polish furniture on damp days, as the moisture in the air will prevent you from obtaining a high gleam.

Dusting Cloth

See **Dusting Cloth for Polished Wood**

High Gleam

To get a really high gleam on finely polished furniture such as pianos, apply your usual polish and sprinkle a small amount of cornstarch (cornflour) on top. Rub until all the polish is absorbed by the cornstarch, leaving behind a high gleam.

Homemade Polish

Mix equal quantities of methylated spirits, vinegar (white vinegar for light colors, malt (brown) vinegar for darker colors) and olive oil. To every $2\frac{1}{2}$ cups (20 fl oz/625 ml) of this mixture, add 1 tablespoon kerosene and mix well. Shake frequently while using. Only polish small areas at a time.
(⊗ *Methylated spirits,* ⊗ *Kerosene*)

Varnished Furniture

Test first on an inconspicuous area to ensure that the finish is really varnish and not some other type of lacquer which could be damaged.

Mix 1 tablespoon dishwashing detergent with 2 tablespoons fairly warm water and add sufficient borax to make a paste. Rub the paste all over the varnish and wipe off with a damp cloth. Finish off with furniture polish. (*Borax*)

 FURNITURE POLISH

Carpet

As quickly as possible, absorb excess liquid. Sponge with diluted laundry detergent and then with clean water. If any stain remains, sponge with methylated spirits followed again with diluted detergent. Finally, sponge with clean water and pat dry. (*Methylated spirits*)

Clothes

Sponge the stain with undiluted laundry detergent and rinse in clear water. If any stain remains, sponge with methylated spirits followed again by laundry detergent. Rinse off. (*Methylated spirits*)

G

GLASS OVENPROOF DISHES

Sprinkle baking soda (bicarbonate of soda) over the bottom of the dish, cover with boiling water and leave for 10 minutes before washing as usual.

This should remove all stains, however, for stubborn stains, rub with a damp cloth dipped in baking soda (bicarbonate of soda) or a piece of fine dry steel wool dipped in salt.

GLASSES STUCK TOGETHER

Immerse the bottom glass, up to three-quarters of its height, in hot water. This should expand the bottom glass sufficiently to release the top glass. If the glasses remain stuck, put cold water or ice cubes in the top glass while the bottom one is in the hot water.

 GLASSWARE

Dull Glassware

Make a paste of baking powder and water and then rub it all over the glassware. Rinse in clean water and dry and polish with a soft cloth.

☛ Fill dull glassware with potato peelings and top off with water. Leave for 2 days, wash as usual.

☛ Fill with cold, black tea, leave for 15 minutes, then rinse with cold water. Dry with a soft cloth.

Gleaming Glassware

Glassware will really sparkle if you add some starch, diluted to a thin paste as per instructions on the packet, to the washing water.

 GLOBE: SHATTERED

Removal

First, switch off the electrical current. Remove the jagged pieces of glass with a pair of pliers, then press a cork bigger than the base of the globe onto the base and turn. The base should pop out.

 GLUE

Cellulose

CLOTHES

Use nail polish remover or cellulose lacquer thinners to soak the stain. Then wash as usual.

(⊗ *Nail polish remover,* ⊗ *Lacquer thinners*)

61

Liquid

CARPET

Lightly soak the stain in a solution of 2 tablespoons laundry detergent, 1 tablespoon white vinegar and 2 cups (16 fl oz/500 ml) warm water. Pat dry, and if necessary, repeat the process.

Water-Based

CLOTHES

Warm water will usually remove water-based glue. However, if stains are stubborn, soak them in white vinegar before washing the item as usual.

 ## GRASS

Sponge the stain with methylated spirits.
($\otimes$ *Methylated spirits*)

Colors

Make a solution of glycerin and paraffin and sponge it over the stain. Leave for 1 hour and wash as usual.

Washables

Dampen the stain with water and cover with sugar. Roll up and leave for 1 hour. Wash as usual.

Whites

Make a solution of 1 tablespoon ammonia and 2 cups (16 fl oz/500 ml) water and sponge it over the stain. ($\otimes$ *Ammonia*)

 ## GRAVY

See **Blood**

 ## GREASE

Asbestos Cement (Fibro)

Make a solution of 2 tablespoons hydrochloric acid to 2^1/2 cups (20 fl oz/625 ml) water. Clean using an old paintbrush and rinse off. ($\otimes$ *Hydrochloric acid*)

Carpet

Mix equal quantities of block magnesia and fuller's earth with hot water. While still hot, spread the mixture over the stain and allow to dry. Brush well and vacuum the carpet.

☞ Liberally sprinkle cream of tartar or baking soda (bicarbonate of soda) over the stained area and leave for 24 hours. Brush or vacuum off.

Cement

See **Oil, Engine**

Clothes

While grease is fresh, sprinkle the stain with talcum powder. Leave for 30 minutes and then brush off.

If the stain is stale, soak it overnight in kerosene. Next day, wash the item in very hot water with laundry powder. (⊗ *Kerosene*)

Cotton

Rub dry powdered starch or cornstarch (cornflour) over the stain and press with a medium-hot iron. Brush off the starch and wash as usual.

Hot Grease

Pour cold water over spilt hot grease. This will set it and prevent it from spreading or soaking in.

Overalls, Coveralls

Soak overnight in a solution of 2 tablespoons epsom salts; (or $^1/_4$ cup (2 fl oz/60 ml) ammonia; or $^3/_4$ cup (6 fl oz/180 ml) kerosene; or 1 cup (8 fl oz/250 ml) white vinegar for light colors, brown vinegar for dark colors), and 1 gallon (4 L) hot water. Next day, wash and rinse as usual.

(⊗ *Ammonia*, ⊗ *Kerosene*)

Painted Woodwork

Make a solution of starch and water and paint it over the stain. When dry, wipe off with a soft cloth.

Paper
Place blotting paper over the stain and press with a warm iron.

Polished Wood
Try rubbing lightly with kerosene. If unsuccessful, make a solution of 2 teaspoons vinegar (white for light colors, malt (brown) for darker colors) to 1 cup (8 fl oz/250 ml) warm water. Dab the solution on the stain and remove immediately. Repeat a few times but do not let the solution remain on the wood. Finish with a cream furniture polish. (⊗ *Kerosene*)

Skin
Rub the stain with cloth or cotton wool that has been soaked in baby oil.

Suede Shoes
Rub the stain with rolled oats, brush it off with a suede brush, and then rub the stain with turpentine. (⊗ *Turpentine*)

Unwashables
Lightly rub the stain with methylated spirits. (⊗ *Methylated spirits*)

Vinyl
Carefully scrub the stain with methylated spirits. (⊗ *Methylated spirits*)

Wallpaper
Mix fuller's earth and methylated spirits to a creamy paste. Spread a thick coat over the wallpaper and leave for 24 hours. Wipe off. (⊗ *Methylated spirits*)

☛ Mix talcum powder with dry-cleaning fluid to a creamy consistency. Spread a thick coat over the wallpaper and leave for 24 hours. Wipe off.

Walls
Wash off with turpentine. Alternatively, use sugar soap. (⊗ *Turpentine*)

Washables
Clean with eucalyptus oil and wash as usual.

 GREEN STAINS

Bathtub or Sink
Soak a cloth in a solution of 2 parts ammonia to 1 part water. Place cloth over stain. Place a weight over the cloth to hold it in place and leave for 1 hour or more. The green stain will now have turned blue, but unlike the green stain, the blue one is washable with dishwashing detergent and water. Repeat if necessary. ($\otimes$ *Ammonia*)

WARNING

Never use steel wool on a bathtub or sink.

 GUM: CHEWING GUM, BUBBLE GUM

Wet the gum thoroughly with methylated spirits, kerosene, turpentine or egg white and lever off with a fairly dull steel chisel or knife. It may require repetition. ($\otimes$ *Methylated spirits,* $\otimes$ *Kerosene,* $\otimes$ *Turpentine*)

Clothes
Treat as for **Chewing Gum, Hair**

Fur
On the inside of the garment, rub the gum with an ice block. When the gum is frozen, it can be broken off.

Hair
Soak a cloth in eucalyptus oil and sponge off the gum.

Small Articles
Wrap the item in a plastic sheet and place it in the freezer. When the gum is frozen, simply lever it off.

H

 ## HAIR RINSE (DYE)

Carpet

Mix 1 teaspoon methylated spirits with 4 drops ammonia. Rub the mixture well into the stain and sponge over with a commercial carpet shampoo.
($\otimes$ *Methylated spirits*, $\otimes$ *Ammonia*)

HANDBAGS

Leather

Use saddle soap according to the manufacturer's directions.

Mesh

Sprinkle white vinegar onto a soft cloth and rub it over the bag. Next, sprinkle ammonia onto another cloth and rub it over the bag. When clean, wipe over the bag with a cloth dipped in water and then let the bag dry before buffing with a dry cloth.
($\otimes$ *Ammonia*)

☞ If the bag is small, place in a suitable container and cover with methylated spirits. Leave for 1–2 hours then remove and buff dry with a soft cloth. Repeat if necessary. ($\otimes$ *Methylated spirits*)

Straw (Colored)

Treat the same as **Straw (Natural)** (below), but instead of lemon juice, use 1 tablespoon water.

Straw (Natural)

Beat 1 egg white until stiff then, while still beating, gradually add the juice of 1 medium-size lemon and 1 teaspoon epsom salts or cooking salt. Using a toothbrush, brush the mixture all over the bag, wipe over with a damp cloth to even out the coating, and leave in the sun to dry.

Vinyl or Plastic
Use undiluted antiseptic. Apply with a cloth and rub until clean. Dry with a clean cloth.

☞ Place a small amount of toothpaste on a damp cloth and lightly rub it over the bag. Wipe clean with a dry cloth.

 ## HANDS

General Cleaner
Add sufficient water to rolled oats to make a thick paste. Rub the paste over your hands until clean and rinse off in cold water.

Rough Hands
Rub hands with white or malt (brown) vinegar and continue rubbing until vinegar dries.

 ## HEAT MARKS

Polished Wood
Mix linseed oil and pumice powder into a thin paste. Rub in the direction of the grain, wipe off with linseed oil. Follow with furniture polish. Repeat if necessary.

 ## HEM MARKS
Rub with white vinegar and leave to soak. Press with a warm iron over a cloth dampened with vinegar.

Delicates
Make a solution of 1 teaspoon white vinegar and $^1/_2$ teaspoon borax to 1 cup (8 fl oz/250 ml) hot water Mix well, immerse ironing cloth, and wring the cloth thoroughly. Place the cloth over the hem marks and press with a warm iron. When dry, brush off any powdery deposit. (⊗ *Borax*)

67

Heavy Coats, etc.
First, rub the marks with fine sandpaper before using vinegar as above.

Velvet
Use a damp cloth under the iron and finish off by brushing against the pile.

HONEY
If the stain is fresh, use warm water to remove any residue. If the stain is old, dab with laundry detergent and rinse with warm water.

HOT PLATES
See **Stove Top/Hot Plates**

I

ICE CREAM
See **Cream, Ice Cream**

INDOOR PLANT MULCH
Coffee grounds are a good mulch for indoor plants.
See also **Fertilizers for Plants**

INK

Ball Point
CLOTHES
Sponge the stain with methylated spirits. When clean, wash with warm soapy water and rinse well. (⊗ *Methylated spirits*)
☞ Wet a cloth with white vinegar, dip into baking soda (bicarbonate of soda) and rub into stain.

VINYL AND UNWASHABLES

Mix equal parts of bleach and methylated spirits. Add enough of this mixture to fuller's earth to make a paste. First, test an unseen part of the fabric with the paste in case it fades. Then rub the paste over the stains and leave to dry. Remove powder residue and rub over with a damp cloth. When dry, rub in some glycerin. ($\otimes$ *Bleach,* $\otimes$ *Methylated spirits*)

☞ Rub the stain with eucalyptus oil.

Fluid

BARE WOOD

Sprinkle on salt and rub with lemon juice.

CARPET

Cover well with dry salt while stain is fresh. As the salt absorbs the ink, brush off and replace with fresh salt. Finally, sponge the area with sour milk followed by methylated spirits. ($\otimes$ *Methylated spirits*)

☞ Saturate the stained area with white vinegar and mop up with a sponge or blotting paper until the carpet is thoroughly dry. Repeat if necessary.

CLOTHES

Soak the item in a weak bleach solution for 20 minutes. Wash as usual. ($\otimes$ *Bleach*)

☞ Spread mustard over the stain. Leave for 24 hours, sponge off with cold water and wash as usual.

COLORS

Soak the stain in sour milk overnight and wash as usual. If unwashable, finish off by sponging.

HANDS

First, rub the stains with white or malt (brown) vinegar and then with salt. Wash hands as usual.

MARBLE

See **Coffee, Marble**

PAPER

Make a solution of 1 part water and 2 parts bleach. Paint onto the stain and blot immediately.

POLISHED WOOD

Immediately absorb excess ink and treat the stain with furniture polish. If the stain has lightly penetrated the surface, try rubbing with pumice powder and a cloth dampened with linseed oil. If successful, finish off with a cream furniture polish. If unsuccessful, the surface will have to be refinished.

WHITES

Wet the stain, then sprinkle on salt and rub well with a slice of lemon. Leave for 1 hour. Rinse and wash as usual.

PERMANENT PRINT

To remove print, such as from calico bags, soak in kerosene for a few hours. Wash as usual.

(⊗ *Kerosene*)

See also **Print, black**

PRINTERS

Squeeze lemon juice through the stain and rinse off. If the ink is stubborn, pour glycerin through it. Wash as usual.

INSECT SPRAY

Washables

Make a mixture of 1 tablespoon borax and 2$\frac{1}{2}$ cups (20 fl oz/625 ml) warm water. Soak the stain overnight, then wash as usual. (⊗ *Borax*)

IODINE

Sponge the stain with a solution of 3$\frac{1}{2}$ tablespoons sodium thiosulfate ("hypo") with 3$\frac{1}{2}$ tablespoons water until stains are removed. Rinse off solution with clean water. (⊗ *Sodium thiosulfate*)

✳ IRON: DRY OR STEAM

Cleaning Base

Spread toothpaste, white or malt (brown) vinegar or silver polish over the base of the iron. Make sure that none of this enters the steam holes. Finish off with a clean cloth dipped in methylated spirits.
(⊗ *Methylated spirits*)

☛ For nonsteam irons, rub the base with fine steel wool dipped in pumice powder or whiting. Finish off as above.

Cleaning Hot Iron

Sprinkle salt on a clean piece of paper. Run hot iron over salt, wipe the iron clean and continue ironing.

J

✳ JAM

Unwashables

Dab the stain with warm water containing ammonia or borax. (⊗ *Ammonia*, ⊗ *Borax*)

Washables

Soak in a mixture of 4 tablespoons borax to $2^{1}/_{2}$ cups (20 fl oz/625 ml) warm water. Wash as usual.
(⊗ *Borax*)

✳ JEWELRY

Cameos

Clean with warm water and dishwashing detergent applied with a soft brush. Rinse and dry well.

Crystal

Make a solution of 1 teaspoon ammonia to $2^{1}/_{2}$ cups

(20 fl oz/625 ml) hot water. If possible, immerse jewelry and leave to soak for 10 minutes. If jewelry cannot be soaked, wash with a soft cloth dipped in the above solution. Rinse in warm water and dry thoroughly. Finally, dip in cologne and dry with a soft cloth. ($\otimes$ *Ammonia*)

Diamanté
Rub gently with a silver-polishing cloth.

Diamonds
Toothpaste or shaving cream applied with an old toothbrush will clean diamonds thoroughly. Rinse off in cold water and then dip in cologne and dry with a soft cloth.

Emeralds
Immerse in tepid, soapy water and rub with fingers. As emeralds are soft stones, do not use a brush. Dry with a soft cloth.

Gilt
Wash in tepid, soapy water and dry with a soft cloth.

Gold
Same as for Diamanté and Diamonds.

Ivory
Sprinkle methylated spirits onto a soft cloth and rub it over the ivory. Finally, soak in a medium-strength solution of bleach for at least 1 hour, then rinse well and wipe dry. Sunlight helps to prevent ivory from yellowing. ($\otimes$ *Methylated spirits*, $\otimes$ *Bleach*)

Marcasite
Same as for Diamanté. Keep away from heat, as this damages the sparkle of marcasite.

Pearls
Same as Gilt but do not leave to soak too long, as you could damage the thread.

Pearls (Cultured), Turquoise

Place in a small container and cover with powdered magnesia. Stir well to ensure that the pearls are thoroughly covered and leave overnight. Then shake off powder and wipe with a soft cloth.

Pearls (Imitation)

Same as real pearls, but handle carefully to prevent damaging the thin coating.

Rubies, Sapphires

Clean in tepid soapy water with a very soft brush. Dry with a soft cloth.

Silver

See **Silver**

✳ JUG: ELECTRIC

Fill the jug three-quarters full with cold water, add a sliced lemon, bring to a boil and switch off. Let stand for about 5 hours. Discard lemon slices and water, and boil with fresh water once or twice to remove any traces of lemon.

K

✳ KETTLES

Cast Iron and Aluminum

Fill the kettle almost full with boiling water. Add 1 tablespoon borax or cream of tartar and boil for approximately 15 minutes. Leave to cool, drain, and remove any residue with dishwashing detergent and steel wool. Wash and rinse thoroughly with boiling water. Repeat if necessary. (⊗ *Borax)*

KETCHUP

Thoroughly wet the stain with cold water and then rub with laundry detergent. Finish off with clean cold water. If the stain is stubborn, dilute borax with warm water and rub it over the stain. (⊗ *Borax*)

KNIVES

Pour a small amount of dishwashing detergent onto a fine pad of steel wool and rub it across the knife blade from the top of the blade down toward the cutting edge. Finish off by wiping the blade with lemon juice and then rinse with clean water.

L

LACE

Crisp Finish

Dip a pressing cloth in a solution of 1 tablespoon borax to 2$\frac{1}{2}$ quarts (2.5 L) hot water. Wring out the cloth, place it over the lace and press with a hot iron. (⊗ *Borax*)

Yellow

Mix 2 teaspoons borax with 5 cups (40 fl oz/1.25 L) cold water in a saucepan. Put the lace in the solution and slowly heat but do not boil. When all the yellow has disappeared, remove from the heat, rinse well and place in the shade to dry. (⊗ *Borax*)

LAMINATED BENCH AND TABLETOPS

Light Stains

Rub with a rag dipped in olive oil or lemon juice.

Moderate Stains

Make a thick paste of baking soda (bicarbonate of soda) and water and rub it into the stain. Leave the paste for at least 2 hours then wipe off. Repeat if necessary.

Heavy Stains

Cut a sheet of the finest grade, wet-and-dry emery paper into pieces, each about 4 x 4 in (10 x 10 cm) in size. Soak the pieces in a solution of soap and water for approximately 10 minutes. Then, while keeping the emery paper saturated with solution, rub all over the laminated surface until the stains are removed. To restore the high gloss dulled by the emery paper, see **Polishing** (below).

Polishing

After washing and drying the laminated surface, rub in a thin coat of silicone car polish. When dry, polish well and apply another thin coat of polish. Again, when dry, polish well. This should result in a really high gloss. However, if not satisfied, repeat the procedure.

✸ LAMPSHADES

Parchment

To 2$\frac{1}{2}$ cups (20 fl oz/625 ml) warm water, add 1 teaspoon laundry detergent and 2 teaspoons methylated spirits. Mix well and gently rub over the lampshade with a damp sponge. Wipe off with a clean sponge dipped in water and place the lampshade on the lamp to dry. For quicker drying, switch on the lamp. When dry, apply a thin starch solution with a sponge. This will keep the lampshade clean for much longer and make cleaning easier next time. (⊗ *Methylated spirits*)

Plastic

Sprinkle antiseptic onto a clean cloth and wipe it over the lampshade. Wipe dry with a clean cloth.

✻ LEATHER

Cleaning

A good general cleaner for leather is saddle soap. Rub the soap in well with a damp sponge and when the leather is clean, dry off with a soft cloth. Alternatively, use one of the following:

- petroleum jelly
- 1 tablespoon vinegar (white vinegar for light colored and malt (brown) vinegar for darker colors,) and 1 tablespoon ammonia diluted with $3^3/4$ cups (30 fl oz/900 ml) warm water. (⊗ *Ammonia*)
- Eucalyptus oil
- $^1/2$ teaspoon borax mixed with $2^1/2$ cups (20 floz/ 625 ml) warm water. (⊗ *Borax*)

Apply any of the above with a clean cloth or sponge.

Do's and Don'ts

- Never use hot water on leather as it could distort and shrink.
- Never use furniture polish, waxes, paraffin, shellac or varnish.
- Do not saturate leather with water.
- When cleaning or polishing, rub briskly but not hard.
- Clean leather at least once a month and do not let dust accumulate.

Restoring

Dip a cloth in linseed oil, glycerin or castor oil and briskly rub it over the leather after cleaning. Rub in one direction only to avoid streaking.

LINEN

Yellowed

Wrap a cheesecloth (muslin) around crushed eggshells in a bundle and boil it with the linen in a small amount of water. When the linen is white, remove it from the water and then wash as usual.

LINOLEUM OR VINYL

Maintenance

Mix together equal quantities of kerosene, methylated spirits and ammonia. Immerse a large cloth in the above solution, let soak for 5 minutes, then, without wringing, hang on a clothesline in the shade to dry completely. To use, rub the cloth over the polished linoleum floor as required.
(⊗ Kerosene, ⊗ Methylated spirits, ⊗ Ammonia)

Polish

To make linoleum really gleam, rub linseed oil over it, let stand for 30 minutes, and then wipe dry.

Removing Layers of Polish

Sprinkle turpentine all over the linoleum and rub well with a rag or an old mop. Clean off the turpentine and old polish with hot water. (⊗ Turpentine)

Removing Stains

Sprinkle kerosene on a pad of fine steel wool and rub over the stains. Clean off with warm water and dishwashing detergent. (⊗ Kerosene)

LIPSTICK

Rub the stain lightly with white vinegar or eucalyptus oil on a moistened cloth.

Washables

Rub glycerin onto the stain and leave for

30 minutes. Sprinkle powdered laundry detergent or ammonia on the stain and wash as usual. (⊗ *Ammonia*)

M

 MARBLE

Cleaning and Rejuvenating

Mix together the following:

- 1 part fine pumice powder
- 2 parts washing soda
- 1 part fine powdered chalk
- 1 part white vinegar
- sufficient water to make a paste

Rub the mixture all over the marble with a soft cloth and when clean, wash off with dishwashing detergent and water.

Any small imperfections can be sanded off with fine wet-and-dry emery paper. Soak paper in water for 10 minutes, wrap it around a cork sanding block and rub gently in the direction of the grain only. Keep immersing the paper in water to prevent buildup of marble dust.

Light Surface Dirt and Grime

Sprinkle turpentine onto a clean cloth and wipe it over the marble. Wash off with warm water and dishwashing detergent and if still not quite clean, rub gently with pumice powder and water. Wash off with clean water. (⊗ *Turpentine*)

Heavy Surface Dirt and Grime

Make a solution of 1 part hydrochloric acid to

5 parts water and apply to the marble with an old brush. Leave to soak for 15 minutes, then rinse off with clean water. ($\otimes$ *Hydrochloric acid*)

Polishing

First, clean the marble as suggested above then, with a soft cloth dipped in a combination of automobile paint-cutting and polishing compounds, rub the marble along the grain in one direction only. Let dry, then buff well with a soft, clean cloth. Finally, apply a commercial silicone-based liquid floor wax and polish well.

MASCARA

Mix a small amount of white vinegar with water and dab it onto the stain. Then rub it lightly with liquid laundry detergent. If the item is washable, rub some eucalyptus oil well into the stain and then wash as normal in warm water.

MATTRESSES

To freshen up an old mattress, sprinkle a mixture of baking soda (bicarbonate of soda) and aromatic talcum powder over it. Leave for about 1 week and then use a vacuum cleaner to remove the powders.

MEDICINES

Dilute the stain with a small amount of warm water and sponge with diluted liquid dishwashing detergent. Pat dry. If unsuccessful, consult the pharmacist.

MENDING: INVISIBLE

Small tears can be quickly repaired by applying a few drops of clear nail polish to both sides of the tear and holding the sides together until stuck. If this method is used carefully, the repair will be virtually invisible and will stand up to washing.

For larger tears or small holes, cut a matching piece of material slightly larger than the tear or hole from the inside of a seam or cuff and cut out a similar-size piece of polythene plastic material or iron-on tape. Turn the garment inside-out, place the piece of plastic on the tear and place the matching material on top of the plastic. With a very hot iron, press the patch until the plastic melts and holds the material in place. Finally, apply a small amount of clear nail polish around the edges of the hole to stop any tendency to lift. Wash normally.

☞ Cut a slightly oversize patch of matching material. Turn the garment inside out, place on a flat surface and saturate the material around the hole with egg white. Apply the patch over the hole and press firmly until the egg white is dry. Smooth out any wrinkles with a warm iron. Wash as usual.

 ## MILDEW

For a general mildew remover, mix the following:
- 4 oz (125 g) powdered starch
- $\frac{1}{2}$ cup (4 fl oz/125 ml) lemon juice
- 4 oz (125 g) soft soap (available from pharmacies)
- $\frac{1}{4}$ cup (2 oz/60 g) common salt

Apply mixture to the stain and leave in open air for 2 hours. Wash and rinse well.

Books

Immerse cheesecloth (muslin) in a solution of 2 tablespoons copper sulfate and $2\frac{1}{2}$ cups (20 fl oz/ 625 ml) water and hang to dry. When the cloth is completely dry, rub it over the books thoroughly.

This method will not damage the books and the cloth can treat approximately 50 books before it requires re-treatment. (⊗ *Copper sulfate*)

Brick or Stone

First, remove the loose mildew with a wire brush. Then mix 3 tablespoons copper sulfate to 1 gallon (4 L) water and rub it over the mildew. Repeat until mildew is removed. Sometimes, after this treatment, a bluish bloom is evident, but this will fade when exposed to rain. When completely dry, the surface may be painted. ($\otimes$ *Copper sulfate*)

China

If the mildew is very deep and on old, delicate china, it is best to get professional restorers to treat it. However, if the mildew is not too deep, rub petroleum jelly over the stain and leave in a cool oven overnight. Next day, wash and make sure the china is thoroughly dry, as mildew can only grow in wet conditions.

Holland Blinds

Rub damp salt thoroughly over the stain. When dry, brush off the salt and wipe over the blind with a damp cloth.

Leather

Rub a liberal amount of petroleum jelly over the stain. Leave for 1 hour and then wipe dry.

☛ Mix 1 part hydrochloric acid with 8 parts water and, using an old paintbrush, brush the mixture over the mildew and hose off.

($\otimes$ *Hydrochloric acid*)

See also **Leather**

Leather Books

Sprinkle ammonia onto a clean cloth and wipe away mildew. ($\otimes$ *Ammonia*)

Washables: Colors

Soak the stain in sour milk and then leave to dry in the sun. Wash as usual.

Washables: Whites

If the mildew is fresh, wash the stain with soap and water. If it is an old stain, squeeze lemon juice onto the stain followed by salt. Leave in the sun to dry then wash as usual.

See also **Mold**

 ## MILK

Cement

Spread wet sand over the stain. With a flat sandstone block, rub the stain until it disappears. If stubborn, a small amount of fresh lemon or lime juice mixed with the sand will help. Do not use ordinary soap powders.

Marble

See **Cream, Marble**

Polished Wood

Wipe up the excess and treat with furniture polish. If still stained, treat as for **Alcohol: Spirits**.

Unwashables

Sponge the stain with methylated spirits and when dry, clean with warm water. ($\otimes$ *Methylated spirits*)

Washables

Soak the item in warm water and wash as usual. If stubborn, sprinkle on borax and soap powder and pour hot water through the stain. Rub gently, leave for 10 minutes and then wash as usual.

 ## MIRRORS

To clean, crumple a sheet of newspaper into a ball, wet it thoroughly with water, wring out as much water as possible and wipe it over the mirror. To dry, simply crumple another sheet of newspaper into a ball and wipe it over the mirror.

Mirror Clouding

Mix together an equal quantity of methylated spirits and glycerin and store it in a glass jar. When required, simply dip a cloth in this mixture and rub it over the mirror. To dry, wipe over with a dry cloth. ($\otimes$ *Methylated spirits*)

✳ MOHAIR

Mohair will retain its softness if you add 4 tablespoons baby shampoo to the washing water. If using the washing machine, turn the garment inside out to minimize damage.

✳ MOLD

Bathroom

Small amounts of mold in the bathroom can usually be removed by brushing the mold with white vinegar.

See also **Shower Curtain; Shower Recess**

Bathroom Mats

Hang up after use to dry to avoid mold forming.

Books

Dilute $1\frac{1}{2}$ tablespoons antiseptic with a small amount of hot water and wipe over the external surface of the book. Wipe dry.

For book pages, sprinkle talcum powder in between the pages and leave for 1 week. Remove the powder with a brush and vacuum cleaner.

Canvas

Make a strong solution of salt, white vinegar and water. Brush the solution well into canvas. Leave in the sun to dry. If required, repeat the procedure.

Kitchenware

To remove mold from kitchenware, soak in a

M

solution of 1 oz (30 g) washing soda to 4 cups (32 fl oz/1 L) hot water. Leave to soak for about 1 day, then rub with a soft type of scourer. Rinse well. To maintain cleanliness of kitchenware, rinse them — every week or so — in a small amount of bleach diluted with an equal amount of water. (⊗ *Bleach)*

WARNING:

Do not immerse kitchen appliances in water. Wipe over with a cloth soaked in the above solution. Keep all cords safely away from water.

Leather

Remove mold by wiping well with saddle soap. When clean, shine the leather by rubbing it with colorless shoe polish. As a precaution, and to help prevent mold returning, never store leather in plastic bags or covered, as this does not allow it to breath.

See also **Leather**

Refrigerator and Rubber Seals

Wipe rubber seals with a cloth soaked in white vinegar. Repeat every 2–3 weeks. If any marks remain on the seals, wipe methylated spirits over them. To prolong the reappearance of mold, wipe the cleaned seals with a thin smear of petroleum jelly. (⊗ *Methylated spirits)*

Shower Curtains

The hem on the bottom of a shower curtain is the perfect place for mold to form, so cut it off for a long-term solution. To remove mold, if a hem is preferred, gather the shower curtain and soak the bottom end in a 1-gallon (4 L) bucket of warm water mixed with 1 cup (8 fl oz/250 ml) bleach. Every few hours, swirl the bottom of the shower curtain in the bleach solution. After a day or so, discard the solution and rinse the bottom of the curtain thoroughly. ($\otimes$ *Bleach)*

Shower Recess

With a shower frame, mold usually forms under the side and bottom seals, and it is best to replace these seals. However, you can try brushing diluted swimming pool chlorine (about 2 parts pool chlorine to 1 part water) into the seals, leave for 10 minutes and then wash off. ($\otimes$ *Swimming pool chlorine)*

Walls in Home

Make a mixture of 1 part bleach to 2 parts water and apply with an old brush to the walls. Leave for about 20 minutes then clean off with fresh water.

Avoid mold on internal walls by having rooms well ventilated. Also, check the external side of the wall to ensure that the damp course at the bottom is above ground level and in good condition. Any fracture allows dampness to rise.

To clean dampness from internal walls that are washable, wipe them with white vinegar or bleach, leave for 15 minutes and then wipe off with a damp, clean cloth. If the wall is not washable, sprinkle the surface with a heavy application of talcum powder and when dry, remove powder with the vacuum cleaner using a brush attachment. ($\otimes$ *Bleach)*

Wardrobes

If you live in an area that is affected by copious amounts of rain and you have a problem with mold on your clothing and shoes, try leaving on a small electric globe in the wardrobe. The extra warmth helps to prevent the formation of mold. As shoes seem to be more easily affected, place them on top of a layer of charcoal in a shoe box. It also helps to leave the wardrobe doors open for 15 minutes every

M

day. On the outer surfaces of wardrobe walls, remove mold by cleaning with a solution of 2 teaspoons white or malt (brown) vinegar to 2 cups (16 fl oz/500 ml) water. Wipe dry and polish with good furniture polish.

MUD: DRY

Heavy Fabric
Rub with the cut edge of a raw potato.

Light Fabric
Wash in ammonia and water, and then rinse well. ($\otimes$ *Ammonia*)

MULBERRY

Hands
Rub stains with green mulberries and wash with warm water.

MUSTY SMELLS

Books
Remove any obvious mold from the covers with a small amount of dishwashing detergent on a cloth. Wipe over them with lavender or eucalyptus oil.

Clothing
Place clothing in the clothes dryer for approximately $1\frac{1}{2}$ hours to remove the musty smell.

Rooms
Half-fill a bowl with baking soda (bicarbonate of soda) and leave it in the room. Replace the baking soda about once a month, as it helps to prevent mold from forming.

N

 ## NAIL POLISH

Clothes

Carefully, without spreading the stain, sponge with nonoily nail polish remover or acetone. Clean the remaining smear with methylated spirits and pat dry. ($\otimes$ *Acetone*, $\otimes$ *Nail polish remover*, $\otimes$ *Methylated spirits*)

WARNING:

Some synthetic materials may be damaged by nail polish remover. Test on an inner seam for suitability.

Polished Wood

Mix equal quantities of vinegar and olive oil and rub onto stain with a cloth dipped in warm water. May require repeated rubbing. When the stain has been removed, restore the surface of the polished wood by polishing with a mixture of equal parts of linseed oil and turpentine. ($\otimes$ *Turpentine*)

Prevent Chipping

Nail polish will adhere better if you dip your fingernails into white vinegar before applying the polish. Do not wipe off the vinegar, but allow it to dry naturally.

Quick-drying Nail Polish

After applying polish, dip fingernails in icy cold water for approximately 2 minutes. The polish will dry very quickly.

 ## NAILS BREAKING

Reduce the tendency for fingernails to break by rubbing them with pure honey. Leave for 10 minutes and wash off.

NONSTICK PANS

You can buy special nylon pads for cleaning nonstick pans, however a piece of nylon netting crumpled up into a ball and used with dishwashing detergent will also do the job.

For badly burnt-on food, sprinkle baking soda (bicarbonate of soda) over the bottom of the pan and cover it lightly with bleach. Let soak for 5 minutes, then add a small amount of water and let boil for 10 minutes. Wash as usual. ($\otimes$ *Bleach*)

 NYLON AND RAYON

Sewing

Stop nylon from slipping and improve machine feeding by rubbing wet soap along the fabric where you are going to sew. Let dry before sewing.

Whiten and Deodorize

Add 2 tablespoons methylated spirits to both the washing and rinse water. ($\otimes$ *Methylated spirits*)

 Add 4 tablespoons baking soda (bicarbonate of soda) or borax to cold or warm water and soak the garment. ($\otimes$ *Borax*)

O

 OIL

Blankets

Mix 1 tablespoon borax and 1 tablespoon soft soap in 2 gallons (8 L) water. Soak blankets for 24 hours.

Rinse well and hang to dry without wringing. (⊗ *Borax*)

CAUTION:

Use only a plastic, glass or porcelain-enamel container to soak the blankets.

Bricks

Add enough whiting to methylated spirits to make a thick paste. Saturate the oil stain with pure methylated spirits, then apply a liberal amount of the thick paste and let dry. When dry, brush off the dried paste and wash off any remaining white residue with clean water and a stiff brush. Repeat if necessary. (⊗ *Methylated spirits*)

Carpets

Liberally sprinkle the stained area with cream of tartar and leave for 24 hours. Brush off or remove with a vacuum cleaner.

Clothes

While the stain is still fresh, sprinkle on talcum powder. Leave for 30 minutes and brush off.

Clothes (Old Stains)

Work from the outer edge of the stain and rub in glycerin. Let soak for 1 hour. Sponge off with a solution of warm water and laundry detergent.

Marble

See **Cream, Marble**

Shoes

Cleaning fluids will remove oil stains, but they also remove some of the coloring and leave an obvious spot. Instead of fluids, dab rubber cement on the stain and smooth it down with your finger. When dry, rub off the rubber cement. This may have to be repeated a number of times, but there will be no spot left behind.

OIL: ENGINE

Cement

If the oil is fresh, sprinkle a liberal amount of dry cement over it and brush in well. As the cement absorbs the oil, replace with fresh cement and continue until the stain is absorbed.

If the stain is dry, mix some caustic soda with very hot water and brush all over the stain well. Let soak for 30 minutes and wash off. Follow with a treatment of dry cement as suggested above.
($\otimes$ *Caustic soda*)

Clothes

If the stain is fresh, sprinkle talcum powder over it. Leave for 30 minutes and brush off. If the stain is old, soak it overnight in kerosene. Next day, wash the item in very hot water with your usual laundry powder. ($\otimes$ *Kerosene*)

 OIL: LINSEED

Linseed oil, if left on too long, may become sticky and difficult to remove. However, a cloth sprinkled with kerosene and rubbed over the sticky surface will assist in removing it. ($\otimes$ *Kerosene*)
See also **Oil**

 ONION ODOR

Add 1 teaspoon white vinegar to the washing water.

 OVEN

Cleaning

While the oven is warm, place a cloth saturated with ammonia inside it and close the door. When cool, the grease will wipe off. If you do this once a week, your oven will stay clean. ($\otimes$ *Ammonia*)

Door Glass
Sprinkle baking soda (bicarbonate of soda) onto a wet sponge and rub it over the glass. Wipe off with a clean cloth.

P

 PAINT

ENAMEL

Carpet
Dab the paint spot with turpentine to soften it. Peel off the paint and sponge with a solution of 1 teaspoon laundry detergent, 1 teaspoon white vinegar and 4 cups (32 fl oz/1 L) warm water mixed together. Pat dry. ($\otimes$ *Turpentine*)

Cement
Make a solution of 1 cup (6 oz/180 g) caustic soda to 2$\frac{1}{2}$ cups (20 fl oz/625 ml) hot water. Spread on the paint spots and let soak for about 5 hours. Wash off. Repeat if necessary. ($\otimes$ *Caustic soda*)

Linoleum and Vinyl
Using hot water, dissolve starch into a paste and apply to the paint spot while hot. Leave for 30 minutes and wipe off.

Skin (Sensitive or Child's)
As kerosene or turpentine may be too harsh for sensitive skin or a child's skin, saturate a piece of cotton wool with baby oil and gently rub over the paint spots. Wash off.

Slate
Paint on a liberal amount of paint remover and, to

prevent evaporation, cover with wet paper or dry blotting paper. Leave for 30 minutes then scrape off with a wire brush. Finally, clean with kerosene. If unsuccessful, apply a solution of 2 tablespoons hydrochloric acid to 2 cups (16 fl oz/500 ml) water then wash off. If still unsuccessful, grind off the paint spots with a Carborundum stone. (⊗ *Paint remover*, ⊗ *Kerosene*, ⊗ *Hydrochloric acid*)

Steel
Clean using paint thinners. (⊗ *Thinners)*

Textured Bricks
Apply a commercial brand of paint remover with an old paintbrush. Wait approximately 5 minutes and then scrape off with a wire brush. Repeat if necessary.

Washables
Soften the paint with glycerin, then make a solution of equal parts of turpentine and ammonia and sponge over the stain. Wash as usual.
(⊗ *Turpentine*, ⊗ *Ammonia)*

Wooden Floor
Mix together $1/4$ cup (2 fl oz/60 ml) turpentine with $1/2$ cup (4 fl oz/125 ml) ammonia and place on paint spots to soften them. Dip a piece of steel wool into the mixture and rub the softened paint spots until they disappear. (⊗ *Turpentine*, ⊗ *Ammonia)*

Odor
Place a bucket of cold water containing 3 chopped onions in the center of the room for a few hours.

PAVING
Washables
Rub the front and back of the paint spot well with cold cream. Do this for approximately 10 minutes, with continual replenishment of the cream, then spread a thick layer over the spot and leave for 24 hours. Wash as usual.

PLASTIC
Clothes
Soak with water and then rub the stain gently using a toothbrush dipped in a mixture of salt and hot water. If the paint is too hard, soak it first in methylated spirits before applying the above salt and water treatment. ($\otimes$ *Methylated spirits*)

 ## PAINTWORK
Homemade Cleaner
Make up a solution of 2 tablespoons methylated spirits to $2^{1}/_{2}$ quarts (2.5 L) water and sponge it over the paintwork. Test on an inconspicuous area and, if too severe, increase the amount of water. An alternative to methylated spirits is acetone.
($\otimes$ *Methylated spirits,* $\otimes$ *Acetone*)

 Mix equal quantities of ammonia and warm water and sponge over the paintwork.
($\otimes$ *Ammonia*)

PASPALUM GUM
Apply eucalyptus oil with a brush. When dry, brush off with a stiff brush.

 ## PASTE
Wallpaper
If paste has stuck to the front of the wallpaper, remove it by placing a sponge dipped in warm water over it. Repeat 2 or 3 times, after which the softened paste should come off by gently rubbing it with a dry cloth.

 ## PASTRY CUTTER
Remove the serrated metal strip from an aluminum foil dispenser box or similar. Form into the shape desired and fasten the ends with sticky tape.

PENCIL: INDELIBLE

Cotton or Linen

Rub the front and back of the stain with butter. After 30 minutes, soap well and wash in warm soapy water. Rinse well. If still stained, rub with methylated spirits and wash as usual.

($\otimes$ *Methylated spirits*)

Wood

Make a mixture of lemon juice and salt and rub it into the stain. Leave for 5–10 minutes to dry and then wash off.

 ## PERFUME

Clothes

Rub the stain with glycerin until removed and wash as usual.

Wood or Lacquer

Dampen tissue paper with acetone or nail polish remover and gently rub the stained surface. Keep the tissue moving, as damage may occur if it is left in the one spot.

($\otimes$ *Acetone,* $\otimes$ *Nail polish remover*)

 ## PERSPIRATION

Odor

Dissolve 2 noncolored aspirin tablets in water and sponge the solution over the area. Hang to dry. Wash as usual.

☛ Sponge the area with lemon juice or white vinegar diluted with a small amount of water. Hang to dry. Wash as usual.

☛ On synthetic materials, sponge the area with a solution of 4 tablespoons baking soda (bicarbonate of soda) and $2^{1}/2$ cups (20 fl oz/625 ml) cold water. Wash as usual.

Shirts, Cuffs and Collars

Soak shirts in a strong solution of epsom salts and water. Then, fill a separate tub with warm water, add cloudy ammonia and soak shirts for 30 minutes. Wash as usual and dry in the sun. If the stain is still evident, rub on lemon juice, leave for 30 minutes, rinse off in warm water and allow to dry in the sun. ($\otimes$ *Ammonia*)

 Sponge the stain with hydrogen peroxide and leave in the sun for about 1 hour.

($\otimes$ *Hydrogen peroxide*)

Unwashables

Sponge with a weak solution of methylated spirits. ($\otimes$ *Methylated spirits*)

Washables

Sponge with a weak solution of white vinegar or ammonia and wash as usual. ($\otimes$ *Ammonia*)

Woolens

Mix 2 teaspoons borax with $1\frac{1}{4}$ cups (10 fl oz/ 300 ml) warm water and sponge over the stain. ($\otimes$ *Borax*)

☆ PEST REMOVAL

Ants

Sprinkle borax on shelves. Place slices of lemon, fresh or stale, along the paths traveled by ants. Rub kerosene on woodwork around windows, doors and base boards (skirting boards). Paint the inside of kitchen cupboards with a solution of 1 tablespoon alum dissolved in 2 cups (16 fl oz/500 ml) hot water. ($\otimes$ *Borax,* $\otimes$ *Kerosene*)

 Sprinkle infested areas with pepper.

Cockroaches

Make up a mixture of 3 parts boric acid, 3 parts

sodium fluoride, 1 part icing sugar and 2 parts cocoa powder. ($\otimes$ *Boric acid*, $\otimes$ *Sodium fluoride*)

Put the mixture in areas frequented by cockroaches such as behind hot-water heaters, under the kitchen sink and in dark storage areas. Replace mixture as required.

Paint the inside of kitchen cupboards with a solution of 1 tablespoon alum dissolved in 2 cups (16 fl oz/500 ml) hot water.

Fleas

Sprinkle carpets and floors with a liberal amount of cooking salt. Leave for 10 minutes and then remove with a vacuum cleaner.

Flies

Rub your skin with a few drops of lavender oil, or with a moisturiser to which a few drops of lavender oil has been added.

☛ Rub your face with petroleum jelly or moisturiser to which a few drops of citronella essential oil have been added.

☛ Rub your skin with a mixture of 2 tablespoons epsom salts dissolved in 2 cups (16 fl oz/500 ml) water.

☛ Sprinkle the inside of the garbage bin with borax. ($\otimes$ *Borax*)

☛ Rub paraffin oil or ammonia on the framework around windows and doors. ($\otimes$ *Ammonia*)

☛ Fresh mint on the table or in a vase near a window will help to keep flies away.

☛ A sponge dipped in boiling water and then sprinkled with a few drops of lavender essential oil and left in the middle of a room will also help to keep flies away. Replenish water once or twice a day, and lavender oil every 4 days.

☞ Heat some cloves in the oven for approximately 15 minutes and place in a saucer near an open window.

Mice

SETTING TRAPS

Always wear rubber gloves when setting a mouse trap to avoid leaving the smell of a human on the trap.

WASHING TRAPS

After catching a mouse, wash the trap in soap and water and rinse well to get rid of the smell of the dead mouse.

BAITS

• A pumpkin seed appears to be very attractive to mice.

• A plump raisin also works well.

• A piece of bread crust flavored with vanilla is usually successful.

Mosquitoes

Rub skin with a few drops of lavender essential oil.

☞ Rub your face with some petroleum jelly or moisturiser to which a few drops of citronella essential oil have been added.

☞ Basil growing in a pot and placed near an open window is very effective in deterring mosquitoes.

Moths

Sprinkle a few drops of ammonia onto a piece of cloth and leave it in your wardrobe. Brush cracks, joints and crevices in furniture, wardrobes and cupboards with 1 tablespoon alum dissolved in 2 cups (16 fl oz/500 ml) hot water.

(⊗ *Ammonia*)

Silverfish
Treat the same as for **Ants** or **Moths**.

 PEST-REPELLING PLANTS IN THE GARDEN
To help keep away insect pests, grow these pest-repelling herbs in the garden.
Ants: Mint, tansy
Aphids: Chives, garlic
Fleas: Fennel, tansy
Fruit Flies: Basil
House Flies: Basil, chamomile, mint, rue, tansy
Mosquitoes: Chamomile
Vegetable Beetles: Oregano, wintergreen
Vegetable Fly: Rosemary, thyme
Vegetable Moth: Dill, hyssop, rosemary

PEWTER
Cleaning and Polishing
Make a paste of whiting mixed with a small amount of linseed oil and rub it over the pewter. When the stains are removed, wash with soap and water (not detergent) and polish dry with a soft cloth.

To prevent stains recurring, wash with soap and water every 3–4 weeks.

PHOTOGRAPHS
Sprinkle a few drops of methylated spirits onto a clean, soft cloth and gently rub it over dirty photographs. ($\otimes$ *Methylated spirits*)

PIANO
Keys
To clean and whiten piano keys, try one of the following methods.
1. Add sufficient hydrogen peroxide, methylated spirits or lemon juice to some whiting to make a

paste and rub it over the keys. Leave for about 1 hour, wipe off, and then rub the keys with undiluted hydrogen peroxide.
(⊗ *Hydrogen peroxide,* ⊗ *Methylated spirits*)

2. Saturate a soft cloth with methylated spirits or cologne, dip it in talcum powder or powdered milk and rub it over the keys.
(⊗ *Methylated spirits*)

3. If the discoloration of the keys is bad, the best thing you can do is to remove them, one by one, and rub them with very fine wet-and-dry emery paper. Soak the emery paper in water for 10 minutes or more, wrap it around a cork sanding block and gently rub each key in the direction of the grain only. Dip the emery paper and cork in water frequently. When clean, wipe dry each key, replace, and apply some liquid floor polish. Buff well.

Musty
Make a small bag from netting, fill it with mothballs and hang it inside the piano.

PIPES AND DRAINS

Kitchen or Laundry Sink
Pour a solution of 5 tablespoons borax to 2$\frac{1}{2}$ cups (20 fl oz/625 ml) boiling water down the sink.
(⊗ *Borax*)

☞ Pour a strongly brewed black coffee down sink.
☞ Pour hot salted water down sink every week.

PLASTIC

Machine Sewing
Place waxed paper on the plastic where you are going to sew. Attach it to the plastic with sticky tape, and when sewing is finished, tear off the paper.

POTS, PANS, DISHES
See **Burns: Pots, Pans, Dishes**
See **Nonstick Pans**

 PREWASH STAIN REMOVER
Mix together the following solution:
- 1¼ cups (10 fl oz/300 ml) hydrogen peroxide
- 1 cup (8 fl oz/250 ml) methylated spirits
- 5 tablespoons cloudy ammonia
- ¼ cup (2 fl oz/60 ml) glycerin

Store in a well-sealed bottle and apply to stains 30 minutes before washing. Wash as usual.
(⊗ *Hydrogen peroxide,* ⊗ *Methylated spirits,* ⊗ *Ammonia*)

☛ Moisten the stained area with cold water and sprinkle sugar on it. Leave overnight and next day, wash as usual.

 PRICE TAGS AND LABELS
Stick-on price tags cannot always be removed cleanly. To remove any residue from the adhesive, rub it lightly with 1–2 drops kerosene or eucalyptus oil on a cloth. (⊗ *Kerosene*)

 PRINT: BLACK
Sugar or Flour Bags
Saturate the printing with kerosene and leave for 30 minutes. Mix laundry detergent with cold water and soak the bag for at least 24 hours. Finally, rub the print to remove it and rinse thoroughly in cold water. Hang to dry. Repeat if necessary.
(⊗ *Kerosene*)
See also **Ink, Print**

R

✴ RAINCOATS

Make a solution of 2 tablespoons ammonia to $2^1/2$ cups (20 fl oz/625 ml) warm water. Sponge the solution over the stained area and hang to dry. ($\otimes$ *Ammonia*)

☞ Cut a raw potato in half and rub it over the stains.

☞ If the raincoat is made of gabardine, heat salt in the oven and rub it over the stains.

✴ REFRIGERATOR
Odor

Cut a lemon in quarters and squeeze the juice from 3 pieces into a bowl of water. Place the remaining piece unsqueezed in the water. Leave the bowl in the refrigerator and renew each week.

☞ Leave an open bottle of vanilla extract or a cut lemon in the refrigerator.

✴ RUBBER HEEL MARKS

Squeeze toothpaste on a soft cloth and rub it over the marks.

✴ RUGS
Afghan

Make a solution of $2^1/2$ cups (20 fl oz/625 ml) cold water, $2^1/2$ cups (20 fl oz/625 ml) white vinegar, 3 cups (24 fl oz/750 ml) methylated spirits and $1/3$ cup (3 oz/90 g) salt. Place the rug on a flat surface and gently apply the solution with a brush until the rug is soaked. Stretch the rug into shape and place clean weights all around to hold it. When dry, remove the weights and lightly brush the rug with a soft, dry brush. (⊗ *Methylated spirits*)

Cashmere and Llama

Wash the rug as you would a woolen garment. Use only washing detergent made for woolen garments, and use only warm water to wash and rinse.

 # RUST

Bath

Mix baking soda (bicarbonate of soda), lemon juice and salt into a paste and rub over the stains. Wash off.

☞ Mix hydrogen peroxide and cream of tartar into a creamy paste. Spread onto the stains and leave for 10 minutes, then rub lightly and wash off. Clean as usual. (⊗ *Hydrogen peroxide*)

Cotton and Linen

Wet the stain thoroughly with water and dab on a small amount of hydrochloric acid. Wash in warm, soapy water. (⊗ *Hydrochloric acid*)

Enamel Surfaces

Mix $^1/_4$ cup (2 fl oz/60 ml) white vinegar, $^1/_4$ cup (1 oz/30 g) all-purpose (plain) flour and $^1/_2$ cup (4 fl oz/125 ml) hydrogen peroxide into a fairly thick paste and spread over stain. Leave for a few hours. Wash off with cold water. (⊗ *Hydrogen peroxide*)

Marble

First, clean the marble as suggested for **Fruit Stains**, then apply the following poultice: Add sufficient whiting or flour to a commercial rust-reducing chemical available to make a paste. Let dry and wipe off.

Nickel

Coat with petroleum jelly and leave for 4 days. Clean off with a cloth dipped in ammonia. (⊗ *Ammonia*)

Polished Metal

Scrape off the rust with a copper scraper to avoid scratches. Do not use abrasive paper or a steel knife.

Scissors

Dip a piece of fine steel wool in kerosene and rub it over the scissors until the rust is removed. Prevent further rusting by rubbing kitchen scissors with a few drops of vegetable oil or other scissors with mineral oil. Remove the oil before next using the scissors. ($\otimes$ *Kerosene*)

Sinks

Cut a lemon in half, dip the raw edge in salt and rub it over the stains. Rinse off immediately with clean water.

☛ Sprinkle white or malt (brown) vinegar onto a cloth and rub it over the stain. Rinse immediately with clean water.

Steel Knives

Remove most of the rust with steel wool and finish off by rubbing both sides of the knife with a cut raw onion. Leave the knife covered in onion juice for about 1 hour. Wash well and resharpen.

Tin (Pots, pans and dishes)

If the rust is very light, simply rub a damp cloth dipped in baking soda (bicarbonate of soda) over it.

☛ Cut an onion in half and rub the raw edge over the rust. Leave for 20 minutes and repeat if necessary. Wash and dry as usual. Rub again with a raw onion to prevent rust recurring.

Tools

Mix 1 tablespoon ammonium citrate in 2$\frac{1}{2}$ cups (20 fl oz/625 ml) water. Soak the tools in the mixture for 24 hours, then rinse with water and smear tools with oil. ($\otimes$ *Ammonium citrate*)

Washables

Mix equal portions of cream of tartar and salt. Wet material and rub in well. Leave in the sun to dry. Wash as usual.

 If the stain is stubborn, boil the fabric in a mixture of 2 teaspoons cream of tartar and 2½ cups (20 fl oz/625 ml) water. Rinse well.

Woolens

Squeeze lemon juice over the stain and cover with salt. When dry, brush off the salt. Repeat if required. Wash as usual.

S

 ## SALTWATER

Clothes

Remove encrusted salt and wash as usual but add 2 tablespoons white vinegar for every 2½ cups (20 fl oz/625 ml) of washing water.

SCORCH MARKS

Carpet (Light-colored)

Make the following solution:
- 1¼ cups (10 fl oz/300 ml) bleach
- 5 tablespoons lemon juice
- 1 cup (8 fl oz/250 ml) water

Sponge the solution over the scorch mark and repeat until the mark fades. ($\otimes$ *Bleach*)

Colors

Dampen the scorch mark and thoroughly rub in some cornstarch (cornflour). Leave to dry and iron as usual.

Nylon, Wool or Mohair

Sponge the scorch mark with diluted hydrogen peroxide (1 part hydrogen peroxide to 4 parts water), then wash in warm soapy water with a small amount of borax added. Ensure that all borax is rinsed off. (⊗ *Borax*, ⊗ *Hydrogen peroxide*)

Unwashables

Make a solution of 1 teaspoon borax to $1\frac{1}{4}$ cups (10 fl oz/300 ml) hot water and spread it over the mark. Sponge off with clean water. (⊗ *Borax*)

Whites

Wet the area with diluted hydrogen peroxide (1 part hydrogen peroxide to 4 parts water) and place in sunlight. May need repetition.
(⊗ *Hydrogen peroxide*)

☛ Dampen a cloth in diluted hydrogen peroxide (as above) and place it over the scorch mark. Cover with a dry cloth and press with a medium-hot iron. Never allow the iron to come in direct contact with the cloth soaked in hydrogen peroxide or dampened fabric, as it may cause rust stains. (⊗ *Hydrogen peroxide*)

SCRATCHES

Furniture

Make a solution of 1 part white vinegar to 2 parts olive oil and rub well into the scratch. On dark furniture, use malt (brown) vinegar.

SEASHELLS

Rub the shell with a new pad of dry, fine steel wool. If the shell is very rough, use a few drops of brass polish, and for a high gleam, finish off with a dry pad. To protect final finish, paint with 1 coat of clear shellac.

SEDIMENT

Decanters and Glasses

Add 1 tablespoon salt to 1 cup (8 fl oz/250 ml) white or malt (brown) vinegar and pour into the decanter or glass. Shake well and leave overnight, giving it an occasional shake. Next day, wash and rinse as usual.

☛ Add 1 tablespoon ammonia to 2 cups (16 floz/ 500 ml) water, treat as above. (⊗ *Ammonia*)

 SHARPENING SCISSORS

Cut some fine sandpaper or wet-and-dry emery paper into thin strips with the scissors. The cutting action sharpens the scissors. If sandpaper isn't available, try cutting some fine steel-wool pads in halves.

 SHEEPSKIN AND LAMB'S WOOL

Dry Cleaning Method

Sprinkle liberally with powdered magnesia and rub in well. Roll up tightly and wrap the rolled skin in a sheet of plastic or clean paper and leave for at least 1 week. Unroll the skin, shake well to remove powder and finish off with a stiff clothes brush.

Wet Cleaning Method

LIGHTLY SOILED SKINS

Dissolve wool-wash laundry detergent in warm water, and add 2 teaspoons ammonia. Immerse the skin, agitating gently for 2–3 minutes or until clean. Hang in the shade on a clothesline and, using a hose, rinse off all the soapy water. When all the water has drained, rub olive oil into the back of the skin. When the skin is nearly dry, work the oil into the skin by rubbing it together. When completely dry, fluff the wool by brushing it with a stiff clothes brush. Be careful when handling wet skin as it tears easily. (⊗ *Ammonia*)

HEAVILY SOILED SKINS

Dissolve wool-wash laundry detergent in warm water and add 2 teaspoons each of ammonia, borax and glycerin. When cool, rub well into the skin, working on a small area at a time and wiping up the excess dirty lather before continuing. Hang on a clothes line in the shade and, using a hose, rinse off all remaining dirty lather. Finish off the same as for lightly soiled skins. (⊗ *Ammonia*, ⊗ *Borax*)

See also **Woolens**

 ## SHOE POLISH

Clothes

Scrape off the excess polish and sponge the stain with laundry detergent. Rinse with water and, if any stain remains, sponge with methylated spirits, followed again by laundry detergent as above. Rinse off. (⊗ *Methylated spirits*)

Soften

To soften, add 3 or 4 drops kerosene or turpentine and place the tin in a warm oven for about 10 minutes. To keep it soft, add 3 or 4 drops castor oil and mix well. (⊗ *Kerosene*, ⊗ *Turpentine*)

 ## SHOES

Linen

Rub with a cloth dipped in white vinegar.

Suede

To clean, dip a clean cloth in white vinegar and gently rub it over shoes. When dry, brush well with an old pair of pantyhose.

Bruised or Shiny

Apply a very thin coating of talcum powder and very gently rub it in a circular motion with very fine sandpaper or steel wool. Next, remove any talcum powder by going over the shoes with sticky tape wrapped around your fingers, sticky side out. Finally, brush well with an old pair of pantyhose.

Brushing

Instead of suede brush, use an old pair of pantyhose.

Dusty

Remove the dust by pressing sticky tape over the shoes. Replace the sticky tape as required.

See also **Suede**

Tennis

Shaving cream worked into a lather and applied to tennis shoes with an old shaving brush makes a very good cleaner. Leave until dry and brush off.

White

Apply undiluted antiseptic with a clean cloth and rub it over the shoes. Dry with another clean cloth.

☞ Place a small amount of toothpaste on a damp cloth and lightly rub it over the shoes. Wipe off with dry cloth.

✸ SHOWER HEAD

To clean accumulated deposits of lime, unscrew the shower head from the wall and soak it overnight in white or malt (brown) vinegar. Next day, while still in the vinegar, brush with an old toothbrush, rinse well in clean water and refit.

✸ SHOWER DOORS: GLASS

Dip a soap-filled pad of fine steel wool into white vinegar and rub away all accumulated scum and soap. Rinse off with clean water.

☞ A cloth, dampened with methylated spirits, will also remove the scum and soap.

(⊗ *Methylated spirits*)

✹ SILK

Wash only by hand in warm, soapy water, and rinse in warm water with 1 teaspoon methylated spirits added. Dry on netting stretched across two clotheslines. The methylated spirits enhances the color and helps to restore the silk sheen when ironed. (⊗ *Methylated spirits*)

✹ SILVER

Badly Tarnished

Rub tarnished silver with a cloth dipped in ammonia and whiting. Rinse off in boiling water. Finally, clean with methylated spirits and rub thoroughly to dry. (⊗ *Ammonia,* ⊗ *Methylated spirits*)

Badly Tarnished Small Items

Make a solution of 1 teaspoon salt, 2 teaspoons baking soda (bicarbonate of soda) and $2^1/2$ cups (20 fl oz/625 ml) warm water and mix well. Immerse silver items in mixture and leave until tarnish disappears. Wash in warm water and dishwashing detergent and rub thoroughly to dry.

Cutlery

See **Cutlery, Silver Cutlery**

Jewelry

Clean silver jewelry with toothpaste using a soft brush. Rinse off in warm water and dry thoroughly.

Polishing Cloth

Maintain the gleam on silver by making your own polishing cloth.

Mix together 2 tablespoons ammonia, 1 tablespoon plate powder and 2 cups (16 fl oz/ 500 ml) warm water. Soak a flannelette cloth in the mixture overnight. Next day, hang outside in the shade to drip dry — do not wring.

Rub the silver with this cloth occasionally and it will always be shiny. (⊗ *Ammonia*)

 Soak a flannelette cloth in milk for 30 minutes, then slowly bring the milk, together with the cloth, to a boil. Hang outside in the shade to dry, without wringing. Use as above.

Storing

Prevent silver from tarnishing by cleaning with powdered starch and then placing it in a storage container with 3 or 4 pieces camphor or chalk, or a satchel of silica gel.

Stubborn Stains

On solid silver (not silver plate), most stubborn stains can be removed by rubbing them with an art-gum eraser.

✳ SLIPPERS

Felt

Clean felt or material-type slippers with carpet shampoo. Mix a small amount of shampoo according to the manufacturer's directions and apply to slippers with a nailbrush or toothbrush. Leave to dry in the shade.

✳ SMOKE STAINS

Paint or Wood

Usually, cleaning with a solution of 1 cup (6 oz/ 180 g) washing soda in 1 gallon (4 L) water will be sufficient to remove most smoke stains. Wash off with clean water. Repeat if necessary. Do not attempt to paint over the soot ,as the tarry deposits in the soot will bleed through the paint. To overcome this, paint the stain with shellac or aluminum paint before using ordinary paint. However, clean before any attempt to paint.

☛ Rub on solution of starch and water or fuller's earth and water. When dry, wipe off and wash as usual.

SOOT: CHIMNEY

Put ordinary zinc onto a blazing fire. The chemical vapor absorbs the soot and it goes out the chimney.

SPECTACLES

A small amount of white or malt (brown) vinegar on a clean cloth will make spectacles gleam.

☛ Mix together ½ cup (4 fl oz/125 ml) methylated spirits and 2 teaspoons glycerin and store in a small bottle. To use, sprinkle a few drops onto a soft cloth and then clean and polish the spectacles. The glycerin will help to prevent the spectacles from misting. (⊗ *Methylated spirits*)

STAINLESS STEEL

Wash stainless steel in the usual way, but finish by rubbing all over with bleach followed by methylated spirits or white vinegar. For a really good shine on stainless steel, rub over it with a dry, crumpled sheet of newspaper. (⊗ *Methylated spirits*)

STICKERS RESIDUE

Remove residue from stickers or labels by rubbing with a cloth dipped in turpentine. (⊗ *Turpentine*)

STICKING PLASTER RESIDUE

Polished Wood

Remove the marks with kerosene and rub over the area with vinegar. Dry off and apply furniture polish.

Skin

Rub with a cloth dipped in kerosene. (⊗ *Kerosene*)

✸ STOVE TOP/HOT PLATES

While warm, clean all over with white or malt (brown) vinegar and steel wool. Wipe with warm water and a sponge, then dry with a clean cloth.

✸ SUEDE

Remove stains with a cloth dipped in white vinegar. If the suede has become flat and shiny, rub it lightly with fine sandpaper and then hold it over boiling water. The rising steam will raise the nap on the suede surface, which can then be brushed, in one direction only, with a soft brush. Allow to dry completely before wearing.

See also **Shoes, Suede; Water Marks, Suede**

✸ SUITS OR TROUSERS

Shiny

Make a solution of 1 teaspoon ammonia to $2^{1}/2$ cups (20 fl oz/625 ml) warm water. Sponge the solution well into the shiny suit or trousers and place a damp cloth over the fabric before ironing as usual.
($\otimes$ *Ammonia*)

For dark clothing which is not too shiny, use strained cold tea to dampen the cloth and place the cloth over the shiny fabric before ironing as usual.

✸ SUNSCREEN LOTION

Dilute borax with hot water and dab it onto the stain. If necessary, finish off by dabbing some laundry detergent onto the area. ($\otimes$ *Borax*)

✸ SUPERGLUE

Fresh superglue can be removed by rubbing with acetone or nail polish remover, but you must act quickly. If you delay, it will take much longer and copious rubbing, and still it might not be completely effective. (⊗ *Acetone,* ⊗ *Nail polish remover*)

T

 ## TAR

Car Paintwork
Rub the stain gently with eucalyptus oil.

Hands
Rub the stain thoroughly with lard.

Linen or Cotton
Spread butter on the stain, then stretch the fabric over a pad made from rags. Dab on a small amount of hydrochloric acid and rub around the stain until it is absorbed by the pad. Wash off in gasoline (petrol) then wash in the usual way.
(⊗ *Hydrochloric acid,* ⊗ *Gasoline*)

Woolens
Dab on glycerin and let soak for 1 hour. Wash off with wool-wash detergent and rinse as usual.

TARNISH

Brass
Mix the following solution:
- ¼ cup (2 fl oz/60 ml) white or malt (brown) vinegar
- 1 tablespoon lemon juice
- 1 teaspoon salt

Apply the solution with fine steel wool in straight lines in one direction only. Do not rub crosswise or in circles. Let stand for 20 minutes. Rinse clean and dry.

113

On fine filigree, apply the solution with an old toothbrush or paintbrush. Small items can be left soaking in the solution for 20 minutes. Wash off with hot, soapy water, rinse in clean water and dry.

☛ For severe tarnish, use a solution of 1 part hydrochloric acid to 5 parts water.

($\otimes$ *Hydrochloric acid*)

Apply with an old brush. Wash off with hot soapy water, rinse in clean water and dry.

See also **Brass**

Copper

Mix equal quantities of kerosene and baking soda (bicarbonate of soda). Using fine steel wool, apply the mixture in straight lines. Do not rub crosswise or in circles. Wash off with hot, soapy water, rinse in clean water and dry. ($\otimes$ *Kerosene*)

See also **Copper**

Silver

See **Silver**

 # TEA

Carpet

Mix borax with warm water and rub the affected area with a cloth dipped in this solution. ($\otimes$ *Borax*)

☛ Spread a small amount of glycerin over the stain and leave for 4 hours. Sponge off with methylated spirits. ($\otimes$ *Methylated spirits*)

China

Rub the stain thoroughly with whiting or salt.

Cotton or Linen

Ensure first that the fabric will withstand boiling water.

Spread the stained area over a saucepan or similar, and, from a height of about $1\frac{1}{2}$–3 ft

(45 cm–1 m), pour boiling water through it. When the stain is removed, wash as usual.

If the stain is old, spread a mixture of 1 teaspoon borax to 2$\frac{1}{2}$ cups (20 fl oz/625 ml) water over it. Leave for 15 minutes and wash as usual. ($\otimes$ *Borax*)

Marble
See **Coffee, Marble**

Vacuum Bottle
Make a solution of $\frac{1}{3}$ cup (2 oz/60 g) baking soda (bicarbonate of soda) to 2$\frac{1}{2}$ cups (20 fl oz/625 ml) boiling water. Pour solution into the vacuum bottle and shake well. Leave for 10 minutes. Wash as usual.

Woolens
Mix glycerin with egg yolk, spread the mixture over the stain. Leave for 30 minutes, then wash in warm water.

✸ TEAPOTS

Aluminum
Fill the teapot with boiling water, add 2 teaspoons cream of tartar and stir. Let stand for 4–5 hours. Remove any white residue with soap and fine steel wool. Rinse well.

China
Moisten a cloth with methylated spirits, then dip it in whiting and rub it on the inside of the teapot. Wash and rinse thoroughly. ($\otimes$ *Methylated spirits*)

Silver
Fill the teapot with boiling water, add 1 tablespoon borax and 3 drops bleach. Cover the teapot with a kitchen towel and let stand for 2–3 hours. Wash and rinse thoroughly. Do not allow the solution to spill onto the outside, as it could damage the silver. ($\otimes$ *Bleach*, $\otimes$ *Borax*)

☞ Mix together 2 teaspoons each of baking soda (bicarbonate of soda), all-purpose (plain) flour and white or malt (brown) vinegar and rub the mixture on the inside of the teapot. Let stand overnight and then wash and rinse thoroughly.

☆ TICK REPELLANT

In 5 tablespoons methylated spirits, melt three $^1/_4$ oz (7 g) camphor tablets and mix well. Apply to your pet's skin every 2–3 weeks. In badly infested areas, apply weekly. (⊗ *Methylated spirits*)

✸ TOBACCO

Odor

Pour 1 tablespoon ammonia in a bowl and leave overnight in the center of the room. (⊗ *Ammonia*)

Preventing Odor

Cover the bottom of each ashtray with baking soda.

✸ TOFFEE

Clean off with warm to hot water.

✸ TOILETS

For slight stains, pour the juice of 2 lemons into the toilet bowl and leave overnight. In the morning, if any stain remains, clean with a toilet brush.

To clean stubborn stains pour in $^1/_3$ cup (3 fl oz/ 90 ml) bleach and leave overnight. By morning, all the stains should be gone. (⊗ *Bleach*)

If the stain is still a problem, empty the water from the tank (cistern) and bowl and cover the bottom of the bowl with a thick paste of borax and hot water. Leave for about 2 hours then refill the toilet and flush away the thick paste. (⊗ *Borax*)

To keep the toilet clean, place small pieces of

soap in the tank (cistern). Every time the toilet is flushed, it helps to clean the bowl. Make sure that no pieces of soap hinder the flushing mechanism.

TOMATO
Treat as for **Ketchup**

TOYS
A good general cleaner for toys is dishwashing detergent. Wet a cloth with water and a few drops of detergent and rub it over the toy. Wipe off with a clean cloth and water.

U

UPHOLSTERY
See **Chair Upholstery**

URINE
Carpet
Absorb as much of the excess as possible, then sprinkle warm water over the area. Follow this by sponging the area with a solution of 2 parts laundry detergent, 2 parts warm water and 1 part white vinegar. Pat dry and then sponge with the solution again. Repeat 2 or 3 times. Finally, sponge with clean water and pat dry. Do not allow the carpet to become saturated.

Washables
Sponge the stain with a small amount of ammonia and soak for a few minutes. Rinse and wash as usual. ($\otimes$ *Ammonia*)

117

V

 ## VACUUM FLASKS

Musty

Put 1 tablespoon sugar in the flask and fill the flask three-quarters full with boiling water. Replace lid, shake the flask a few times and leave for 30 minutes. Empty and rinse well in cold water.

 ## VEIL: WHITE BRIDAL

Storing

Before storing, rinse well in an extra-strong solution of washing blue or laundry-whitening preparation. When dry, place waxed paper over it and press with a warm iron. If the veil is bulky, place in a plastic bag, blow bag up and seal it with a rubber band.

 ## VOMIT

Carpet and Unwashables

Pick up excess with rags. Sponge the area with diluted laundry detergent and pat dry. When completely dry and if any stain remains, sponge with methylated spirits. ($\otimes$ *Methylated spirits*)

Odor

Make a weak solution of baking soda and water, and sponge onto the affected area.

W

✳ WALLPAPER

General Purpose Cleaner

Mix together 1$\frac{1}{2}$ cups (6 oz/180 g) all-purpose (plain) flour, 2 tablespoons ammonia, 1 teaspoon baking soda (bicarbonate of soda) and sufficient cold water to make a stiff dough. Place it in a bowl and steam for 1 hour. Knead well and leave for 1 hour. To clean the wallpaper, rub with pieces of the dough. (⊗ *Ammonia*)

☞ Rub the marks gently with an art-gum eraser.

☀ WATER MARKS

Carpet

Do not let the water dry; absorb it with a sponge as quickly as possible. Then, if possible, prop up the carpet to let air circulate and place it near an electric heater or fan. When dry, remove any stains with a diluted solution of commercial carpet cleaner.

Polished Wood

Rub petroleum jelly or camphorated oil into the polished wood. Keep rubbing until the marks disappear.

Silk or Velvet

Hold the fabric over steam for a few seconds and then pat dry.

Suede

When spots are dry, remove them by rubbing with a soft pencil eraser or by rubbing the spots against another part of the suede material.

See also **Suede**

Unpainted Wood

Use a commercial brand of wood bleach in which the use of two liquids is employed.

 Place 3 or 4 sheets of blotting paper over the stain and press with a fairly warm iron. Repeat until the stain is removed.

WAX

Clothes

Place clean blotting paper over the wax and press with a hot iron. Remove the remaining smear with methylated spirits. (⊗ *Methylated spirits*)

See also **Candle Wax**

Floor

Scrub the floor with a mixture of $^1/_3$ cup (3 fl oz/ 90 ml) ammonia, $^1/_3$ up (3 fl oz/90 ml) dishwashing detergent and 1 gallon (4 L) hot water. Wait until completely dry then apply new wax. (⊗ *Ammonia*)

WINDOW GLASS

Newspaper is an excellent, general window glass cleaner and polisher. Use as for **Mirrors**. Stubborn dirt should be scraped off with a razor blade or fine steel wool. Any remaining stain on the glass can be removed with white vinegar.

WINE

Carpet

Absorb the excess liquid as quickly as possible, then sprinkle a liberal amount of talcum powder over the area. Replace the powder as it becomes wet. Sponge with clean water and pat dry. If still stained, sponge with diluted laundry detergent or glycerin, let stand for 30 minutes then sponge with clean water. Pat dry.

☞ Immediately soak with soda water. Mop up with toweling, and repeat the soda water process until all traces of the stain have disappeared.

☞ For smaller spills, sprinkle salt liberally over the spill. Leave until the liquid is absorbed, then vacuum up.

Cotton or Linen

Ensure first that the fabric will withstand boiling water.

Spread the stained area over a saucepan or similar and, from a height of about 1$\frac{1}{2}$–3 ft (45cm–1 m), pour boiling water through it. When the stains are removed, wash as usual.

If the stain is old, spread a solution of 2 teaspoons borax and 1$\frac{1}{4}$ cups (10 fl oz/300 ml) water over it. Leave for 15 minutes and wash as usual.
($\otimes$ *Borax*)

Wool, Rayon or Silk

Wet the stain with cold water followed by glycerin. Let stand for 1 hour, then sponge with lemon juice. Rinse off.

✳ **WOOLENS**

Mix the following solution in a large screwtop jar:
• 2$\frac{1}{2}$ cups (10 oz/300 g) wool-wash laundry detergent
• 1$\frac{1}{4}$ cups (10 fl oz/300 ml) methylated spirits
• $\frac{1}{4}$ cup (2 fl oz/60 ml) eucalyptus oil
• $\frac{1}{4}$ cup (2 fl oz/60 ml) warm water

Add $\frac{1}{2}$ cup (4 fl oz/125 ml) of this mixture to 1 gallon (4 L) warm water. Mix well and gently immerse the woolens. Soak the woolens for 10 minutes, then press and squeeze, without rubbing, until clean. Finally, hang to dry without wringing.
($\otimes$ *Methylated spirits*)

White

Dampen and sprinkle with powdered magnesia. Rub in well, roll up and put into a plastic bag. Leave for 10 hours and then rinse well and dry in the shade.

Removing Pilling (Knobs)

Brush with a flat, plastic pot scourer.

Y

 ## YELLOW STAINS

Washables

Make a bleaching solution of 2 tablespoons hydrogen peroxide to 1 cup (8 fl oz/250 ml) water and sponge the stain until it disappears. Wash as usual.

($\otimes$ *Hydrogen peroxide*)

 ## YOGURT

Rinse the stain under running water and then rub with laundry detergent. Rinse off the detergent.

Z

 ## ZINC CREAM

Remove stains with white vinegar.

INDEX

INDEX

INDEX

127

First published in the UK in 2007 by
Apple Press
Sheridan House

ISBN-13: 978 1 84543 180 8

Set in Frutiger & Giovanni on Quark XPress
Printed in Singapore by Kyodo Printing Co.